Priya Solanki is a sought-after barrister practising at One Pump Court Chambers. She has over 12 years' experience. She has an extensive practice in all areas of immigration (including business immigration), asylum, deportation, trafficking, unlawful detention, EEA and EUSS applications.

She regularly provides in-house training, seminars and webinars for Immigration Law Practitioners Association, Practice Enterprise and other organisations. She has delivered extensive training on the topic of sham marriages and is now often considered by instructing solicitors as a "go-to' person for such cases.

Priya also has a particular interest in and vast experience of cases involving gender violence and vulnerable clients.

Prior to coming to the Bar, she practised in immigration and asylum law as a supervisor and senior caseworker at a not-for-profit organisation. This gives her the great advantage of being able to assist with case preparation before cases reach appeal stage. This combined with her extensive advocacy experience makes her a popular choice.

She has been recommended since 2017 as a Leading Junior barrister in immigration by the Legal 500. The Directories state that "she has a sharp mind and demonstrates excellent client care", "she is tactically astute, good under pressure and very persuasive in court", "she is very knowledgeable in presenting appeals", and that "she has a passion for this area of work".

# A Practical Guide to Challenging Sham Marriage Allegations in Immigration Law

# A Practical Guide to Challenging Sham Marriage Allegations in Immigration Law

Priya Solanki
Barrister

Law Brief Publishing

Published 2021 by Law Brief Publishing, an imprint of Law Brief Publishing Ltd
30 The Parks
Minehead
Somerset
TA24 8BT

www.lawbriefpublishing.com

Paperback: 978-1-912687-93-0

*To my husband, Ritesh, and my children, Simran and Raj, without whom this book would have been completed much sooner. Thank you for your patience and love.*

*To my parents, my sister, Asha, and my aunt, Aruna, for their encouragement.*

*And to all my lovely friends and wonderful colleagues, particularly Gilda Kiai, Kate Nickson and Gemma Wilson, for their assistance and support.*

# PREFACE

The Immigration Act 2014 introduced a new framework for the Home Office investigating sham marriages. With the Home Office investigating thousands of marriages and civil partnerships under the legislation each and preventing several marriages from taking place, it is essential that practitioners in immigration law are familiar with the frameworks for investigating marriages and the complexities of the law in this regard.

In this book, we start by considering the rights of individuals to marry under Article 12 of the ECHR. We then go on to consider the differences and complexities in the definitions of a sham marriage and marriage of convenience. There is detailed analysis of Part 4 of the Immigration Act 2014 and the key changes introduced by this, i.e., the marriage and referral investigation scheme and the impact this has had on the right to marry. We look at the relevant regulations and statutory guidance for Home Office staff. We also consider at length marriage investigations outside of this scheme. Readers are guided through the importance of the UKVI conducting investigations into marriages lawfully and provided with tools to challenge unlawful and irrational decisions. We scrutinise the applicable tests to be applied by decision-makers when making findings and consider the consequences that flow from a bogus marriage finding. This guide explores the most recent and relevant authorities and UKVI Policy Guidance on sham marriages and marriages of convenience.

This book will allow more effective applications to be submitted by practitioners where these issues arise and for better challenges to decisions which raise sham marriage allegations.

The stated law in this book is believed to be correct and up-to-date to 28 February 2021.

Priya Solanki
March 2021

# CONTENTS

# CHAPTER ONE

# THE RIGHT TO MARRY

> "Marriage law . . . goes well beyond its earlier purpose in the common law of legitimising sexual relations and securing succession of legitimate heirs to family property. And it is much more than a piece of paper."[1]

> "Even in these days, when many in British society believe that there is little social difference between marrying and living together, marriage still has deep significance for many people, quite apart from the legal recognition, status, rights and obligations which it brings... It brings legal, social and psychological benefits to the couple when they marry, while they are married and when it ends. Denying those benefits to a couple whose relationship is genuine is neither a rational nor a proportionate response to the legitimate aims of a firm and fair immigration policy."[2]

> "Denying to members of minority groups the right to establish formal, legal relationships with the partners of their choice is one way of setting them apart from society, denying that they are "free and equal in dignity and rights"."[3]

When considering sham marriage allegations in immigration law it is important to remember the right to marry. This right is enshrined in Article 12 of the European Convention of Human Rights which provides that "Men and women of marriageable age have the right to marry and

---

[1] *Minister of Home Affairs v Fourie*, Case 60/04, Constitutional Court of South Africa, para 70, per Sachs J

[2] *Baiai & Ors, R (On The Application of) v Secretary of State For The Home Department* [2008] UKHL 53 [45], [2009] 1 A.C. 287

[3] Ibid. para 44

to found a family, according to the national laws governing the exercise of this right".

The right to marry has been described as a fundamental right, subject only to national laws governing its exercise. It has been made clear that the scope afforded to national law is not unlimited. National laws may lay down formal rules concerning matters such as notice, publicity and the formalities whereby marriage is solemnised. They may also set rules of substance based on generally recognised considerations of public interest; this includes rules concerning capacity, consent, prohibited degrees of consanguinity and the prevention of bigamy. It has been emphasised that national laws governing the exercise of the right to marry must never injure or impair the substance of the right and must not deprive a person or category of person of full legal age and capacity of the right to marry or substantially interfere with their exercise of the right.[4]

However, the Courts have affirmed that the right to marry does not guarantee the right to choose the geographical location of the marriage or a particular legal system for the marriage to be conducted under; see for example, *A v United Kingdom* (1983) 5 EHRR CD296, [1982] ECHR 15 and *Application No 10914/84 v Netherlands* (1985) 8 EHRR 308.

Further, a national law may properly authorise a national authority to delay a proposed marriage between a citizen and a third-country national for a reasonable period to establish whether the marriage is one of convenience and if it is, to prevent it; see for example, *Sanders v France* (1996) 87 B-DR 160, *Klip and Krüger v Netherlands* (1997) 91 A-DR 66 and *O'Donoghue and Others v the United Kingdom* no. 34849/07 ECHR 2010. This is because Article 12 ECHR protects the right to enter only into a genuine marriage.

---

[4] *Hamer v United Kingdom* (1979) 24 DR 5 [60-62]; *F v Switzerland* (1987) 10 EHRR 411 [32]

Article 12 does not apply to the marriage and relationship between spouses or civil partners beyond the right to marry. For example, Article 12 does not oblige a State to facilitate parties to a marriage living together or to remain in a country to found a family: this aspect of family life falls to be examined under Article 8 of the ECHR[5]. A non-genuine marriage will not give rise to family life that may be protected by Article 8 ECHR. Identifying and excluding sham marriages have thus become an increasingly crucial part of the government's project of managing and reducing immigration.

With the above in mind, we will go on in the following chapters to consider the measures that have been put in place in the UK to prevent sham marriages or marriages of convenience.

[5] *Gribenko v. Latvia (dec.) no.*76878/01, 15 May 2003; *Abdulaziz, Cabales and Balkandali v. the United Kingdom* 28 May 1985 Series A no.94 paras. 62, 68); *Savoia and Bounegru v. Italy (dec.)* no.8407.05, 11 July 2006

# CHAPTER TWO

# WHAT IS A SHAM MARRIAGE AND A MARRIAGE OF CONVENIENCE? IS THERE A DIFFERENCE?

In this second chapter, we will consider the definitions of a sham marriage and a marriage of convenience.

The Home Office say that sham marriages pose a significant threat to UK immigration control. They have assessed that around 35,000 marriages and civil partnerships a year involve a foreign national for whom the marriage could be advantageous in immigration terms[6]. They further estimate that between 4,000-10,000 applications are made in a year under EU law on the basis of a sham marriage or civil partnership[7].

The terms 'sham marriage' and 'marriage of convenience' are frequently used synonymously[8]. They are however defined in different terms.

## 2.1 Sham Marriage

A sham marriage is defined under the Immigration Acts as one in which there is no genuine relationship between the parties to the marriage or

---

[6] Home Office (2013) Tackling Sham Marriage Impact Assessment HO0090, page 5.

[7] Ibid. page 2.

[8] Indeed the Home Office specifically and incorrectly say in their Marriage Investigation Guidance Version 4.0 31 December 2020 (pp10, 12) that for immigration purposes the terms are synonymous.

civil partnership, and either one, or both, of the parties enter into the marriage for the purpose of circumventing UK immigration controls[9].

## 2.2 Marriage of Convenience

A marriage of convenience is defined as a marriage entered into for the purpose of circumventing immigration laws[10].

One can see that unlike the former sham marriage term, a couple being in a genuine relationship does not feature in the marriage of convenience definition. This results in a situation where a couple in a long-term, subsisting, cohabiting relationship can be found to be in a marriage of convenience. The case of *Molina, R (On the Application Of) v The Secretary of State for the Home Department* [2017] EWHC 1730 (Admin) dealt with this exact scenario. Mr Molina was a Bolivian national who entered the UK illegally in 2007, in April 2013 he met an Italian national and they entered a relationship, in September 2014 they started to live together and they planned to marry in May 2015. The Secretary of State accepted that theirs was a genuine relationship, she accordingly accepted that this was not a sham marriage but she considered that this instead met the different definition of a marriage of convenience. It was concluded that Mr Molina was rushing to get

---

[9] Sham marriage is defined in statute at Section 24(5)(6) and Section 24A(5)(5A) of the Immigration and Asylum Act 1999, as amended by Section 55(3) of the Immigration Act 2014, and Regulations 12(4)(5) of the Immigration and Social Security Co-ordination (EU Withdrawal) Act 2020 (Consequential, Saving, Transitional and Transitory Provisions) (EU Exit) Regulations 2020/1309

[10] A marriage of convenience is defined in Recital 28 of Directive 2004/38/EC of the European Parliament and of the Council of 29 April 2004; Regulation 2 of The Immigration (European Economic Area) Regulations 2016, S.I. 2016/1052 ('the EEA Regulations') as saved by The Citizens' Rights (Application Deadline and Temporary Protection) (EU Exit) Regulations 2020, S.I., 2020/1209 and The Immigration and Social Security Co-ordination (EU Withdrawal) Act 2020 (Consequential, Saving, Transitional and Transitory Provisions) (EU Exit) Regulations 2020, S.I., 2020/1309, Schedule 3; and Annex 1 of Appendix EU and Appendix EU Family Permit of the Immigration Rules. The EEA Regulations and Appendix EU also refer to durable partnerships of convenience giving these the same definition.

married as he knew that his immigration status would benefit from this union. The High Court agreed with these conclusions, noting the distinctions in the two terms[11].

Fortunately, the High Court's decision in *Molina* was appealed to the Court of Appeal and the matter was settled with the decision of Judge Grubb in the Administrative Court being set aside by consent. The accompanying statement of reasons to the consent order is available online[12] and is worth considering in full. It explains that a genuine couple might decide to wed much sooner than they had originally thought they would owing to immigration reasons but that is not necessarily a marriage of convenience. Some extracts from the lengthy statement of reasons are set out here,

> "57) The Court of Appeal may, therefore, consider that while (per Richard LJ in Rosa v SSHD [2016] 1 WLR 1206, above), the focus is on the intention of the parties, the objective circumstances of a relationship may be a consideration in deciding whether a marriage is one of convenience, because, where a relationship is one that could reasonably be expected to lead to marriage in due course, marrying earlier to secure an immigration advantage may not involve gaining the right or benefit in circumstances that are outside the objective of the measure in question...
>
> 63)However, the officer's conclusion that' this may not be a sham marriage' and her conclusion that there was a genuine relationship of some sort tend to suggest a belief that there was a genuine relationship, albeit that the reason for the parties' rush to marry was to secure an immigration advantage.
>
> 64)In such circumstances, the Secretary of State accepts, on these particular facts, that the fact that Mr Molina and the EEA national

---

[11] Para.64

[12] https://www.freemovement.org.uk/wp-content/uploads/2018/12/20172330-Other-5b05-12-1810.135d5b15d.pdf

> were, in the officer's opinion, rushing to be married might nonetheless be more likely to fall on the side of legitimate advantage-taking, than abuse of rights.
>
> 65) The Secretary of State does not concede, in this appeal, that durable partners cannot, in law, be parties to a marriage of convenience, but he accepts that, on the facts, known to him through the Immigration Officer, the distinction that was drawn between a sham marriage and a marriage of convenience was not sustainable, and that, therefore, the decisions to detain and remove which were taken on the basis of that distinction, did not provide an adequate basis to do so."

One wonders whether it was really intended that couples in genuine relationships be potentially prevented from marrying by this legislation. The Immigration and Asylum Act 1999 itself says that a where there is a genuine relationship between a couple there can be no sham marriage. Throughout Home Office Policy Guidance the terms sham marriage and marriage of convenience are used interchangeably, suggesting they should be approached in the same way.

The success of the appeal in *Molina* provides hope that the expansion of the definition of marriage of convenience will be challenged further. Currently, lawyers will have to continue to battle with the distinction between the terms and advise their clients that are in genuine relationships that they can still be caught out.

## 2.3 The 'Sole Aim' or 'Predominant Purpose' of the Marriage

Whilst there is a difference in the definitions, in both expressions 'the purpose' of the marriage is key. The way in which this purpose has been considered has however changed significantly over the years.

Marriages of course occur for a number of reasons; for example, tradition, love, pregnancy, religion, or indeed to enable a couple to continue and strengthen their family life together in the UK at that time. Would the intentions of a couple in the last example be sufficient to find that this was a marriage of convenience?

Historically, the answer to this question would have been no. Previously, and for quite some time, for a marriage of convenience to be made out the marriage had to be conducted with the 'sole aim' of circumventing the rules on entry and residence[13]. Whilst the couple in the last example are gaining an immigration advantage by marrying, it is quite evident that this is not their sole purpose. A significant reason for their marriage is that they simply wish to be together. These individuals would have been able to refer to *R (On The Application of Baiai and Others)*[14] where the Court said that "the authorities are not free simply to disregard those marriages which they believe have been entered into purely in order to gain some perceived immigration advantage. No doubt such marriages do take place. There is also no doubt that they are difficult to detect, not least because of the difficulty of unpicking the variety of reasons why two people might choose to marry one another. There are many perfectly genuine marriages which may bring some immigration advantage to one or both of the parties depending on where for the time being they wish to make their home. That does not make them "sham" marriages." In coming to this conclusion, the House of Lords referred specifically to the requirement for the 'sole aim' of the marriage to be for an immigration advantage[15].

In July of 2017, the Supreme Court moved away from the 'sole aim' approach in a case called *Sadovska v SSHD* [2017] UKSC 54, [2017] 1 W.L.R. 2926. Despite the court noting that the European Directive[16] and a Communication from the Commission to the European

---

[13] See European Council Resolution 97/C382/01 of 4 December 1997 on measures to be adopted on the combating of marriages of convenience, Article 1; Recital 28 of Directive 2004/38/EC; and *R (On The Application of Baiai and Others) v Secretary of State For The Home Department* [2008] UKHL 53, [2009] 1 A.C. 287 [6].

[14] [2008] UKHL 53, [2009] 1 A.C. 287 [35]

[15] Para.6.

[16] Directive 2004/38/EC, Recital 28

Parliament[17] referred specifically to 'sole purpose' they noted that a 2014 Handbook from the Commission[18] suggested a more flexible approach. Relying on this Handbook, over the Directive, they extended the definition of a marriage of convenience to one where gaining an immigration benefit must be the 'predominant purpose'[19].

The case of *Seferi & Anor, R (On the Application Of) v Secretary of State for the Home Department* [2018] EWHC 287 (Admin) demonstrates the expansion of the definition well. Here, the Secretary of State reached no view on the genuineness of the relationship between the couple. The fact the EU national party to the marriage had admitted to researching how her foreign partner could legalise his stay, albeit that she had not discussed this with him, combined with a reasonable inference that Mr Seferi would know that marriage to an EU national would assist his immigration status was deemed sufficient for the Secretary of State to conclude that the marriage was being entered 'predominantly' for the immigration advantage it would give to Mr Seferi[20].

Practitioners may wonder how the decision in *Seferi* sits comfortably with Lady Hale's words in *Sadovska*, where she said that an overstayer in the UK may be 'delighted to find an EU national with whom [they] could form a relationship and who was willing to marry [them], that does not necessarily mean that their marriage was a "marriage of convenience".'[21]

In the case of *R v IAT, ex parte Arun Kumar* [1986] Imm AR [455] Sir John Donaldson MR commented that 'Any attempt to achieve a delicate

---

[17] A Communication from the Commission to the European Parliament and the Council on guidance for the better transposition and application of Directive 2004/38/EC, dated 2 July 2009

[18] Handbook on addressing the issues of alleged marriages of convenience between EU citizens and non-EU nationals in the context of EU law on free movement of EU citizens, dated 26 September 2014

[19] Para.29.

[20] Para.36.

[21] Para. 35.

and detailed analysis of the motives for the marriage is more likely to obfuscate than enlighten. The motives will often, and perhaps usually, be complex and defy such analysis.' The current authorities show how attempts to analyse purposes and intentions can indeed obscure and complicate the picture resulting in decisions which are difficult to understand. Nonetheless, motives are what must be analysed.

It is important that you and your clients consider and set out all of the underlying reasons that they are marrying. Whilst a couple may say they wish to remain in the UK together, what must be explored is whether it is remaining here or simply being together that is vital for them. The reasons for their decisions should be considered at length and explained with real care.

There may of course not be a predominant purpose for a marriage or civil partnership. Instead a number of equally important objectives may be met through marriage. As Lady Hale said in *Sadovska*, 'incidental immigration and other benefits' are insufficient for a marriage of convenience to be made out[22].

[22] Para.29.

# CHAPTER THREE

# THE HISTORY OF HOME OFFICE REGULATION AND PREVENTION OF MARRIAGES TO MIGRANTS IN THE UK

Before analysing the current systems that the Home Office has in place in the UK to prevent non-genuine marriages and partnerships, it is useful and interesting to consider the previous arrangements that have been in place.

Marriage and relationships present challenges for UK Visas and Immigration in controlling migration to the UK. Over time, several requirements have been introduced into the immigration rules to reduce the flow of spouses to the UK.

From 1980 until June 1997 there was a 'Primary Purpose Rule' (PPR) in place[23]. This imposed a requirement that an applicant needed to show that the marriage was not entered into primarily to obtain admission to the UK, in addition to showing that the parties intended to live together permanently as man and wife. The rule was considered to disproportionately affect South Asians. In 1991, 2872 appeals were determined against refusal of entry clearance as a husband or fiancé, 2709 of these appellants were from the Indian subcontinent[24]. One can see how individuals in arranged marriages, as opposed to pre-marital

---

[23] Statement of Changes in Immigration Rules HC 251, paras 47(a), 50(a), 131(a)

[24] A report by Young Justice, The primary purpose rule: a rule with no purpose, Justice 1993, p17

relationships, struggled to show that their relationship was for other reasons. In 1997 this rule was abolished.

The Immigration and Asylum Act 1999 received royal assent in November 1999. Section 24 instructed registrars to inform the Home Office if they were suspicious of a sham marriage.

In 2003 the immigration rules were changed so that spouses and unmarried partners were granted two years leave to enter or remain as opposed to one year[25]. The White Paper which proposed to extend this probationary period explained that this was done to 'provide a longer period to test the genuineness of the marriage and increase the chance of exposing sham marriages.'[26]

In 2005 the Home Office commenced the Certificate of Approval (CoA) scheme[27]. Under this scheme, individuals subject to immigration control and without indefinite leave to remain had to apply to the Secretary of State for permission to marry before their marriage and they were permitted to marry only at a certain designated registry office. The superintendent registrar could not enter notice of the marriage into the marriage notice book unless they held written permission. There was a fee for the CoA scheme, initially £135.00 and later £295.00. Individuals who held a visa which was issued for no more than 6 months, or who had less than 3 months left on their visa, or who could not show that there were exceptional compassionate circumstances in their case would see their applications for permission to marry rejected. Asylum seekers were not permitted to marry until their claims had been determined. The rules exempted those who married in the Anglican Church.

---

[25] Statement of Changes in Immigration Rules, HC 538

[26] Home Office (2002) Secure Borders, Safe Haven: Integration with Diversity in Modern Britain (UK: The Stationery Office) Cm 5387, at p100

[27] The scheme was operated under the Asylum and Immigration (Treatment of Claimants) Act 2004, s19(3)(b)

The High Court[28] and then the Court of Appeal[29] found that the regime was not proportionate, it constituted a substantial interference with Article 12 ECHR rights, it was discriminatory and violated Article 14 of the Convention. In summary, it was found that the scheme was discriminatory on the grounds of religion and it prevented a large number of genuine couples from marrying. It was considered the purpose of the scheme, which was to prevent abuse of immigration control through sham marriages, could be achieved by measures which did not assume that anyone who was without indefinite leave to remain would be getting married for immigration purposes. In 2007, following these decisions, the CoA scheme was amended.

The CoA scheme was then considered by the House of Lords in *Baiai & Ors, R (On The Application of)* [2008] UKHL 53, [2009] 1 A.C. 287 in July 2008. The Lords considered that the mandatory fee to be paid for a CoA was a positive disincentive to couple who sincerely desired to marry and that it may impair the essence of the right to marry for a needy applicant who could not afford the same[30]. It was found that the scheme was a disproportionate interference with the exercise of the right to marry as it did 'not provide for or envisage any investigation at all, because ... such investigation is too expensive and administratively burdensome. Thus, subject to the discretionary compassionate exception, the scheme imposes a blanket prohibition on exercise of the right to marry by all in the specified categories, irrespective of whether their proposed marriages are marriages of convenience or whether they are not.'[31]

In April 2009 the Home Office stopped charging for CoAs. From July 2009 to July 2010, a procedure was in place which allowed migrants who

[28] *Baiai & Ors v Secretary of State for the Home Department & Anor* [2006] EWHC 823 (Admin), [2007] 1 W.L.R. 693

[29] *Secretary of State for the Home Department v Baiai & Ors* [2007] EWCA Civ 478, [2007] 3 W.L.R. 735

[30] Paras. 30, 40; see also *O'Donoghue and Others v the United Kingdom* no. 34849/07 ECHR 2010

[31] Para. 31

had applied for CoAs between 2005 and 2009 to be able to pay for their fee to be refunded.

On 9 May 2011, almost three years after the House of Lords judgment in *Baiai*, the Certificate of Approval Scheme was abolished[32].

In July 2011, a consultation named 'Family Migration' was published by the Home Office. This showed that in 2010 family migration with a route to settlement in the UK was 114,700. They set out a number of proposals to address this which included;

- introducing a new minimum income threshold requirement for partners,
- extending the probationary period before spouses and partners could apply for settlement from 2 years to 5 years to test the genuineness of the relationship and encourage integration,
- asking local authority social services departments to carry out an assessment of an individual's capacity to consent to marriage when a sponsor of a marriage-based application is a person with learning difficulties or vulnerable,
- defining more clearly what constitutes a genuine and continuing relationship,
- finding an objective way of identifying whether a relationship is genuine and continuing or not.

The document set out indicators that could be taken into account in assessing marriages of convenience and quite significantly set out

[32] The Asylum and Immigration (Treatment of Claimants, etc) Act 2004 (Remedial) Order 2011

proposals for more effective work between the Home Office and General Register office to detect and disrupt sham marriages.

It was these proposals which eventually lead to the system we currently have in place; Appendix FM and FM-SE of the Immigrations Rules[33] and importantly the marriage referral and investigation scheme in Part 4 of Immigration Act 2014[34]. In the next chapter, we will analyse Part 4 of the 2014 Act in some detail.

---

[33] Statement of Changes in Immigration Rules HC 194 13 June 2012

[34] Explanatory Notes Immigration Act 2014, Chapter 22, paras. 28-30

# CHAPTER FOUR

# THE MARRIAGE REFERRAL AND INVESTIGATION SCHEME – IMMIGRATION ACT 2014

At the beginning of March 2015, a referral and investigation scheme was put in place for proposed marriages and civil partnerships across the UK that involve a foreign national who could benefit in immigration terms[35]. The Home Office say that the system is in place to disrupt and deter sham marriages and prevent individuals gaining migration advantages.

The scheme has several parts to it; (a) the referral to the Home Office, (b) the decision to investigate the marriage, (c) the investigation, and (d) the decision on compliance with the investigation. Before we look at these aspects of the system, we will briefly consider the preliminaries to marriage.

## 4.1 Preliminaries to Marriage

In order to marry, there are certain civil preliminaries that must be carried out[36]. Individuals give notice of their proposed marriage or civil

[35] Immigration Act 2014, Part 4; The Referral of Proposed Marriages and Civil Partnerships Regulations 2015, S.I. 2015/123; Please note referral and investigation schemes similar to the scheme in England and Wales discussed in this book have been commenced in Scotland and Northern Ireland, see The Referral and Investigation of Proposed Marriages and Civil Partnerships (Scotland) Order 2015, S.I. 2015/396 and The Referral and Investigation of Proposed Marriages and Civil Partnerships (Northern Ireland and Miscellaneous Provisions) Order 2015, S.I. 2015/395 and Sham Marriage and Civil Partnership (Scotland and Northern Ireland) (Administrative) Regulations, S.I. 2015/404

[36] Marriage Act 1949 Part III; Asylum and Immigration (Treatment of Claimants) Act 2004, ss19-24; Registration of Marriage Regulations 2015, S.I. 2015/207 Part 2; Civil

partnership at their local register office[37]. Giving notice means that they are stating that they intend to get married or enter a civil partnership. Notice must be given in person, each party must be resident in the registration district for a period of seven days prior to giving notice. A fee is payable. The notice states where a couple wish to marry or register their civil partnership and it is valid for 12 months. The couple must provide specified evidence of their name, age, nationality and address when giving notice. From 2 March 2015, a notice to marriage has to be displayed to the public for 28 days before the marriage can occur[38]. An application can be made to reduce that notice period.

## 4.2 The Referral

If one of the parties to the marriage is not an exempt person[39] they need to give notice of marriage together at a designated register office (DRO)[40].

Under Sections 24 and 24A of the Immigration and Asylum Act 1999 there is a duty on a registration officer to report to the Home Office where there are reasonable grounds for expecting that a marriage or civil partnership will be a sham.

However, as of March 2015 a proposed marriage or civil partnership in the UK will automatically be referred to the Home Office by a

Partnership Act 2004, ss8-12; Civil Partnership (Registration Provisions) Regulations 2005, S.I., 2005/3176

[37] Schedule to The Immigration (Procedure for Marriage) Regulations 2011, S.I., 2011/2678, https://www.gov.uk/marriages-civil-partnerships/give-notice

[38] Immigration Act 2014, s 62(1); Marriage Act 1949, s31

[39] Ibid. ss 49, 62(1).

[40] https://assets.publishing.service.gov.uk/government/uploads/system/uploads/attachment_data/file/224796/DROs_GOV_UK..pdf

registration official if it involves an individual who is not an exempt person[41].

The definition of an exempt person has changed with the UK's withdrawal from the EU.

After 1 July 2021 an individual is exempt from the scheme if they are a British national, an Irish national, a person with settled status or pre-settled status under the EU Settlement Scheme (EUSS) a person with a decision pending on an application for EUSS leave submitted prior to 1 July 2021[42], if they hold appropriate immigration status, which means a permanent residence as a result of a retained enforceable EU right[43], if they are exempt from immigration control[44] or are settled in the UK[45].

---

41 Immigration Act 2014, s 48(1)(1A)(1B); Marriage Act 1949, s28H; Civil Partnership Act, s12A

42 The Immigration and Social Security Co-ordination (EU Withdrawal) Act 2020 (Consequential, Saving, Transitional and Transitory Provisions) (EU Exit) Regulations 2020, S.I. 2020/1309 para 20(6)(a)(b) amends Section 62 of the Immigration Act 2014. This definition applies only from 1 July 2021. Up-to and including 30 June 2021 exempt individuals under section 62 of the 2014 Act include a relevant British national, an EEA national or a Swiss national. On 31 December 2020 the Immigration (European Economic Area) Regulation 2016 ('the EEA Regulations') were revoked and EU free movement ended. As a result of this from 1 January 2021 free movement rights under Directive 2004/38/EC cease to have effect in the UK and EEA citizens and their family members will require permission to enter and remain in the UK. EEA nationals, aside from Irish citizens and those with status under the EUSS or a decision pending on an EUSS application that was submitted before 1 July 2021, are brought within scope of the sham marriage referral and investigation scheme.

43 Immigration Act 2014 ss 49(2)(a),(2A)

44 Immigration Act 2014 s 49(2)(b); The Proposed Marriages and Civil Partnerships (Meaning of Exempt Persons and Notice) Regulations 2015, S.I. 2015/122, para.3, i.e., has the right of abode in the UK under section 2(1)(b) of the Immigration Act 1971, is a member of a diplomatic mission or their family member, or is a member of HM forces or of Commonwealth forces undergoing training or visiting forces.

45 Immigration Act 2014 s 49(2)(c); Immigration Act 1971 s 33(2A), i.e. has Indefinite Leave to Enter or Indefinite Leave to Remain.

Individuals are also exempt if they hold a marriage or civil partnership visit visa under the Immigration Rules or they hold fiancé(e) or proposed civil partner leave granted under Appendix FM, Appendix Armed Forces or outside of the immigration rules[46].

An exempt person can be referred to the Secretary of State by a registration official where the official is not provided with specified evidence[47] to show that they are exempt[48]. The decision maker is to satisfy themselves, including based on Home Office records, that the relevant individual(s) are not exempt before deciding to investigate a proposed marriage[49].

### 4.3 The Decision to Investigate

Referrals from registration officers under this scheme are sent to the Home Office Marriage Referral and Assessment Unit (MRAU). Once a referral is made to the Home Office, the Secretary of State has to decide whether or not to investigate the couple.

Under Section 48(3), (4) and (5) of the Immigration Act 2014, the Secretary of State may not decide to investigate the marriage or civil partnership unless she is satisfied (a) that one or neither of the parties is an exempt person and, (b) she has reasonable grounds for suspecting that the proposed marriage or civil partnership is a sham. There is no duty upon the Secretary of State to investigate even when these criteria are made out. The Home Office's operational priorities and resources can be

[46] The Proposed Marriages and Civil Partnerships (Meaning of Exempt Persons and Notice) Regulations 2015, S.I. 2015/122, para 4.

[47] Referral of Proposed Marriages and Civil Partnerships Regulations 2015, S.I. 2015/123, paras. 5, 6

[48] Ibid. paras 5, 6

[49] Immigration Act 2014 – Marriage and civil partnership referral and investigation scheme: statutory guidance for Home Office staff March 2015, page 6.

taken into account. They must however make a decision whether or not to investigate if they receive a referral.

In making a decision to investigate, the Secretary of State must have regard to her published guidance, namely Immigration Act 2014 – Marriage and civil partnership referral and investigation scheme: statutory guidance for Home Office staff March 2015[50]. It is important the requirements are considered carefully as they are very particular and a failure of the Home Office to adhere to these will be challengeable.

The Statutory Guidance explains that in assessing whether there are reasonable grounds for suspecting a sham marriage or partnership, there will be an assessment against immigration records, intelligence and evidence-based risk profiles.

The risk profiles include an individual being recorded as deceased, being an immigration overstayer or absconder, being in breach of their conditions of leave, having entered the UK illegally, being removed from the UK, being an offender or having links to criminality, having previously been suspected of being involved in a suspicious marriage or partnership, having an outstanding application based on their relationship with another spouse/partner, having previously sought leave on the basis of deception or fraud, having previously sponsored or been sponsored by another spouse/partner, having a factor in their immigration history which based on immigration intelligence or enforcement operations gives rise to reasonable grounds to suspect. The Guidance explains that the process will be mainly automated to filter out cases and it will only be cases where there is a need for additional scrutiny which will receive a manual assessment by a decision-maker. It is not the case that the presence of one of the above factors means that the relationship will be investigated; this simply results in additional manual

[50] https://assets.publishing.service.gov.uk/government/uploads/system/uploads/attachment_data/file/419313/Statutory_guidance__March_2015_.pdf

scrutiny of the relationship and an assessment on all of the available information.

The nationality of the individuals is not a relevant factor. However the Statutory Guidance states that if the review of the risk profiling indicates that it would be strengthened by the inclusion of nationality this could change. The Secretary of State would have to give consideration as to whether a Ministerial authorisation was necessary under Schedule 3, Part 4, paragraph 17(4)(a) of the Equality Act 2010.

The Secretary of State must be satisfied that there are reasonable grounds for suspecting that it is a sham before deciding to investigate.

Under Section 48 of the Immigration Act 2014, within the 28-day marriage notice period, the Home Office must make the decision whether or not to investigate and she must give notice of that decision to both parties to the proposed marriage or civil partnership, and to the relevant registration official[51]. If she fails to carry out these steps within the relevant statutory period, any decision made to investigate will not be lawful. The decision to investigate must further be made by an Executive Officer or equivalent or a more senior individual[52].

The Secretary of State's notice of investigation must explain (a) that she will be considering whether parties to the marriage have complied with the investigation, (b) the requirements that the parties may have to comply with and the consequences of failing to comply, (c) the conduct of the investigation, (d) that the marriage or partnership is now subject to a notice period of 70 days, not 28 days, (e) that a decision on the parties compliance with the investigation will be made within this 70-day period, beginning on the day that their marriage notice period began, (f) the date that this 70-day period will end, (g) the possible outcomes of the investigation, (h) the consequences of these outcomes and (g) any

---

[51]s48(7)(8)(9).

[52] Immigration Act 2014 – Marriage and civil partnership referral and investigation scheme: statutory guidance for Home Office staff March 2015, page 9

other information that the Secretary of State considers appropriate[53]. The notice will also inform the parties of their need to notify the Secretary of State of any change in their address during the investigation[54].

Notice of the investigation decision can be given in a variety of ways to the party, their representative and registration officials, including by hand, fax, post, email, document exchange, courier[55].

It is imperative that the 28-day and 70-day notice period are calculated correctly. There can be a challenge to the Secretary of State's decision to investigate and decision on compliance if the decisions are made outside the statutory periods. In England and Wales, the relevant statutory period commences the days after notice is entered in the marriage book or recorded in the register[56].

If the Home Office decides not to investigate whether the marriage or partnership is a sham, the section 48 notice given to both parties and the registration official will allow the marriage to take place after the 28-day notice period so long as the registrar is satisfied that there is no legal impediment to the marriage.

### 4.4 The Conduct of the Investigation

If the Home Office decides to investigate a marriage or partnership, her investigation must be conducted lawfully. The responsibility for

[53] Immigration Act 2014. s 51; The Proposed Marriages and Civil Partnerships (Conduct of Investigations, etc.) Regulations 2015, S.I., 2015/397; Immigration Act 2014 – Marriage and civil partnership referral and investigation scheme: statutory guidance for Home Office staff March 2015, page 10-12

[54] Referral of Proposed Marriages and Civil Partnerships Regulations 2015 (for persons giving notice in England and Wales) S.I. 2015/123 paras.8-9

[55] Proposed Marriages and Civil Partnerships (Meaning of Exempt Persons and Notice) Regulations 2015, S.I. 2015/122, paras.5-7

[56] Immigration Act 2014 – Marriage and civil partnership referral and investigation scheme: statutory guidance for Home Office staff March 2015, page 12.

investigating is that of Immigration Enforcement (IE) Investigation Officers.

The Immigration Act 2014 – Marriage and civil partnership referral and investigation scheme: statutory guidance for Home Office staff March 2015[57] and The Proposed Marriages and Civil Partnerships (Conduct of Investigations, etc) Regulations 2015, S.I. 2015/397[58] set out how an investigation into a proposed marriage or civil partnership should be conducted by an investigation officer for the purpose of establishing whether it is a sham.

Representatives must advise their clients fully of what the investigation will require from them; the requirements are in some respects quite onerous and if an individual fails to meet the terms this can result in a decision that finds they have not been compliant with the investigation thereby preventing the couple from marrying. Equally, if a Home Office investigation does not follow the rigorous procedures and safeguards set out in the Regulations and Guidance there may be a challenge to any decision that follows. For that reason, we will here consider the steps that the Secretary of State and that clients should follow in some detail.

During an investigation, one or both of the parties to the marriage may be required to provide information, evidence or photographs[59] and be interviewed in any of the following circumstances: in person at home[60], in person at Home Office premises in or outside the UK[61], whilst

---

[57] Pages 13-22.

[58] Para 3(1); Immigration Act 2014 s 50(1)(2).

[59] The Proposed Marriages and Civil Partnerships (Conduct of Investigations, etc) Regulations 2015, S.I. 2015/397, Paras. 12, 13.

[60] Ibid. Para 6.

[61] Ibid. Paras. 7, 8.

detained in the UK[62], by telephone, video-link or over the internet[63]. A party can be interviewed more than once[64].

As part of the investigation, each party may be required to provide information or evidence about: themselves and the other party, their relationship with the other party, their living arrangements and those of the other party, their future plans and those of the other party[65]. The Statutory Guidance states that interviews must be conducted in a properly probing but balanced way with questions directed to the genuineness of the relationship and whether the marriage or partnership is a sham[66].

In Chapter 5 of this book we look at the 'Family Policy: Partners, divorce and dissolution' which is used by the Home Office in deciding applications based on relationships under Appendix FM of the Immigration Rules. This sets out factors that are associated with a genuine and subsisting relationship and those which are not. It is certainly worth working through this, as it is likely similar issues will be considered in an investigation.

It is important to note that Home Office requests for information, evidence or photographs must be made in writing. If a requirement for evidence or photographs is imposed during interview, the Secretary of State must follow this up in writing[67]. When asking for these items the investigating officer must: (a) include a description of the information, evidence or photographs that must be provided, (b) set out how the information, evidence or photographs must be provided, such as by post, email or at interview, and include address details, (c) include the date by

---

[62] Ibid. Para 10.

[63] Ibid. Para 9.

[64] Ibid. Para 4(6).

[65] Ibid. Para 3.

[66] at page 17.

[67] The Proposed Marriages and Civil Partnerships (Conduct of Investigations, etc) Regulations 2015, S.I. 2015/397, Paras 12(4)(5).

which the information, evidence or photographs must be received, and (d) in respect of evidential documents – set out the circumstances in which a certified translation or a certified copy may be provided[68]. In relation to electronic documents, individuals can be asked to show these during an interview and the Home Office may make a note of the contents, they may photograph the same, they may request a screenshot of the document, or ask for an email to be forwarded to a specific email account[69].

In order to arrange an interview, a party might be required to contact the Secretary of State in a manner specified in the notice to investigate[70]. A relevant party must be given three working days from the date the section 48 notice is received to make contact. If an individual has received a notice after the date they were to make contact, they will need to prove that the notice was received late[71].

Interviews must be arranged with at least three working days' written notice of the date, place and time. Where agreements have been made for an interview with less than three days' notice that can be arranged[72].

The person required for interview must reasonably make themselves available so that a date and time can be agreed and of course the date for the interview can be no later than the 70-day limit specified in the section 48 notice[73]. Where an interview is to take place with both relevant parties, a person may be required to agree the date and time for interview

---

[68] Ibid. Paras 12(6)(7)(8).

[69] Ibid. Paras 13.

[70] Ibid. Para 5.

[71] The Proposed Marriages and Civil Partnerships (Meaning of Exempt Persons and Notice) Regulations 2015, SI 2015/122, para 7

[72] The Proposed Marriages and Civil Partnerships (Conduct of Investigations, etc) Regulations 2015, S.I. 2015/397 paras. 6(2)(3)(4), 7(2)(3)(4), 8(2)(3)(4), 9(2)(3)(4), 10(2)(3)(4), 11(2).

[73] Ibid. paras. 5(4).

on behalf of the other relevant party so far as this is practicable[74]. Every reasonable effort must be made to accommodate the parties preferred time and date of interviews but where that isn't possible the investigating officer may set an alternative date, place and time[75]. Given the need for the Home Office to make reasonable efforts to accommodate preferred times and date, it is important that issues such as, for example, fixed work commitments, caring responsibilities, medical appointments, are highlighted so that these can be taken into account.

The Regulations state that where a party is unable to attend an interview the investigating officer may decide to rearrange an interview[76]. The Statutory Guidance goes a little further and states that an investigation officer must accommodate a reasonable request to rearrange an interview where this is possible[77]. It follows that good reasons, supported by evidence where possible, must be provided for requests to rearrange. A refusal to rearrange may be irrational in certain circumstances and therefore susceptible to judicial review. Where the Home Office agrees to rearrange an interview, the relevant party or parties may be given less than 3 working days' notice of the date. They cannot however be given less than 24 hours' notice, unless the individuals have agreed to that[78]. The Guidance states that the Home Office will not normally agree to rearrange more than once[79].

An interview must take place during normal office hours, unless the relevant party (or parties) agree that an interview may take place outside normal office hours or if an interview has commenced and been substantially completed during normal office hours it may then continue

---

[74] Ibid. paras. 5(5).

[75] Immigration Act 2014 – Marriage and civil partnership referral and investigation scheme: statutory guidance for Home Office staff March 2015, page 19.

[76] The Proposed Marriages and Civil Partnerships (Conduct of Investigations, etc) Regulations 2015, S.I. 2015/397, Para 11(1).

[77] at page 19.

[78] Para 11(2).

[79] Ibid.

outside normal office hours[80]. "Normal office hours" are between 9.00 am and 6.00 pm, Monday to Friday, excluding Good Friday, Christmas Day or a bank holiday, in the UK[81]. Practitioners may be aware that often interviews that take place at the home of the parties are commenced and largely completed outside of these hours; there may be good lawfulness arguments.

During a home interview, the officers may make observations about and ask the relevant parties about their living arrangements. The Home Office staff conducting the interview must make a signed and dated written record of any observations they have made, but they must also record any reply given by a party to the observations[82]. If an officer has, for example, observed that there are no photographs of the couple in the home they may note this. If the couple have explained that they are shy, or that they keep photographs on electronic devices and do not print them, this should also be recorded. If a written record (and a later decision) suggests that matters have been observed in the home and held against individuals, but that the parties have not been asked to comment upon the arrangements this may be unfair. An investigating officer may ask to see reasonable evidence that the parties cohabit if this is what is being claimed; the officer must again sign and date any written record made of the evidence provided[83]. This means that if a couple are asked to show an officer their bedroom or a bathroom for example, so that they officer can view their living arrangements, this and anything inspected should be recorded. Any written record will need to be considered with care by the parties and their representatives. It may be that the parties are of the view that evidence provided, or that was clearly visible, has not

---

[80] Ibid. paras. 4(8)(9)(10).

[81] Ibid. Para 2; Where an individual is outside of the UK, normal office hours are determined by looking at what is normally regarded as a working day in that particular country or territory.

[82] Ibid. Paras 6(5)(6

[83] Ibid. Paras 6(7)(8).

been recorded. These sorts of points must be raised at an early stage where possible.

For interviews conducted at Home Office premises outside the UK, the relevant party to the marriage must be resident outside the UK and the Home Office premises must be located within a reasonable travelling distance of that individual's place of residence[84]. Reasonable travelling distance is not defined anywhere so advisers will need to think about the distance, time, methods of travel and costs involved and whether a rigorous interview should occur after a particularly long journey. The Regulations do however state that the premises need not be in the same country or territory.

A party detained can be required to attend an interview conducted in person or by telephone[85]. The Statutory Guidance states that attendance at interview should not be a reason to delay an individual's planned removal[86]. We will return in Chapter 6 to enforcement action that can be taken against persons who are referred under this scheme.

At the outset of a telephone interview the investigation officer conducting the interview must identify themselves by name, position and place of work and they must identify the relevant party by name, nationality and date of birth.[87] The officer must telephone the relevant party on the number notified which they have provided to the Home Office and they may telephone the relevant party 30 minutes prior to the time notified to them. The relevant telephone line must be kept free during this period and then during the period of the interview. One can easily envisage issues with signals and reception that could create problems for individuals facing telephone interviews.

---

[84] Ibid. Paras 8(2).

[85] Ibid. Para 10(5).

[86] at page 19.

[87] The Proposed Marriages and Civil Partnerships (Conduct of Investigations, etc) Regulations 2015, S.I. 2015/397, Paras 9(5)(6).

The person conducting the interview must make a written record of it and will provide the party or parties interviewed with a copy of this record if they request it[88]. This record must be completed during the interview, must constitute a verbatim account of what is said or an account of the interview which 'adequately summarises' it, and it must be signed and dated by the person who made it[89]. Where the Home Office provide a record of interview which 'adequately summarises' obvious problems can arise. Summaries can often be imprecise and fail to record detail which might be very important. Where such a summary is provided representatives should analyse whether what has been provided is adequate and if it is not they must explain why this is the case. For these reasons, it is very important that the record is sought promptly, i.e., whilst the parties are able to accurately remember what occurred and raise any complaints about omissions and errors. Unfortunately, there is nothing in the Regulations or the Statutory Guidance that confirms that records will be provided expeditiously or in good time prior to a decision being made. It really does fall upon representatives to press for timely disclosure.

An interviewee may be accompanied at an interview by an appropriate legal representative, i.e. a qualified person within the meaning of section 82 of the Immigration and Asylum Act 1999[90]. Home Office interviews can be very stressful. A lawyer will ensure that proper procedures are followed during the meeting and their presence can ease pressure. There is nothing within the Guidance or the Regulations that provides for a read back of the notes or the parties being able to contemporaneously check an officer's record at the end of interview. It is not uncommon for disputes to arise as to questions asked, answers given and evidence provided. Having real-time agreement from the parties as to the contents of the records would have been a good safeguard. In the absence of this,

---

88 Ibid. Regs 4(14)(17).

89 Ibid. Regs 4(15)(16).

90 Ibid. Regs 4(11)(18); see s 84 Immigration and Asylum Act 1999 for who is a qualified person to provide immigration services

a representative who is present in an interview can make their own verbatim written record which can be used as evidence.

Interviewees may also be accompanied at an interview by an interpreter, appointed by the party if they wish or provided by the Home Office if necessary[91]. Parties and representatives are often uneasy about having an interpreter present as it is not unusual for the Home Office to conclude that the relevant parties to marriage speak in different languages so they must not be able to communicate with each other. Interpreters are permitted for good reason. They can be useful for a variety of reasons, such as anxiety, nervousness with the process or simply the ability to understand more complex words in the English language. The reasons that an interpreter is being requested can be explained to the Home Office to later prevent this being used against the parties. The use of an interpreter does not mean that the parties do not speak English together or another common language. If there are concerns in this regard, the parties or a representatives can suggest that this is established in an interview through some basic questions asked and answered in English.

Interviewees cannot be accompanied at an interview by any other person without the consent of the investigation officer[92]. A party or parties involved in an investigation may be vulnerable for a range of reasons[93] and this might mean that they require additional support through the process. It may well be appropriate in some circumstances for another individual, such as a support worker, to be present.

It can be seen from the above that there can be a lot of scope for challenges to the conduct of investigations.

---

[91] Ibid. Regs 4(12).

[92] Ibid. Para 4(13).

[93] See Safeguarding Vulnerable Groups Act 2006, s 59

## 4.5 The Compliance Decision

Under Section 50(4)(5)(6)(7) of the Immigration Act 2014, within the 70-day period, the Secretary of State must decide whether or not each of the parties to a proposed marriage or civil partnership subject to an investigation under the scheme has complied with that investigation ("the compliance decision"). Her decision must be given to the parties and to any registration official within the 70-day period[94]. The importance of checking the relevant dates is obvious as any decision made or served outside the statutory period is unlawful.

In deciding the compliance issue the Home Office must again have regard to The Proposed Marriages and Civil Partnerships (Conduct of Investigations, etc) Regulations 2015 and the Statutory Guidance.

If the Home Office consider that a party has failed to comply with a requirement to arrange or attend an interview, to provide confirmation of identity or to provide information, evidence or photographs, or to notify the Home Office of a change in address in accordance with the Regulations they may give notice to the party saying that (a) they believe they have failed to comply with a requirement, (b) explaining why they believe that, and (c) giving the party an opportunity to contact the Secretary of State (providing contact details) with a view to complying by a specific date which must give at least three working days' notice[95]. It is not compulsory for the Home Office to provide this opportunity to individuals. If you or your client consider they should have done this prior to making a final compliance decision you will need to show that

---

[94] It is worth noting that the Respondent's Guidance Marriage Investigation Version 4.0 31 December 2020 states at page 17 that an investigation officer must aim to inform a registration officer of an outcome of investigation, with the compliance decision, by the 65th day where possible.

[95] The Proposed Marriages and Civil Partnerships (Conduct of Investigations, etc) Regulations 2015, S.I. 2015/397, paras. 14 and 15

they acted irrationally by failing to do so. Ultimately it is for the parties to show they have complied with the investigation[96].

A failure to reply to questions or a refusal to answer a question or a refusal to answer questions which results in the interview coming to an end, can be regarded as a failure to comply with the interview. Where a party is required to attend by telephone, a failure to keep the telephone number they provide free may be regarded as a failure to comply.[97] A failure of a party to confirm their identity during a telephone interview may also be regarded as failure to comply[98].

A reasonable excuse may exist for non-compliance with a requirement imposed upon a party[99]. In the statutory guidance the following are given as example of when a reasonable excuse exists: (a) where there are compelling, compassionate reasons for failing to comply with the requirement, (b) there are reasons beyond the control of the relevant parties which prevented them from complying with the requirement, or (c) there has been administrative failure by the Home Office[100]. In respect of reasons beyond the control of the parties, often individuals are asked to produce documents from third parties such as landlords and banks. There can be difficulties obtaining this in-time or the documentation being in the format the Home Office request. The parties should explain the problems they have faced and evidence this where possible. The Statutory Guidance explains that all relevant information, evidence, notices and guidance must be taken into account in considering the compliance question and whether there is a reasonable excuse[101].

---

[96] Immigration Act 2014, s 50(3)(4)

[97] Ibid. para 16.

[98] Ibid. para 9(6)

[99] Ibid. para 17(2)(3)

[100] See page 24

[101] See pages 23 and 24

The Marriage Investigation Policy Guidance states that an "inflexible approach to the provision of documents where they would not make a fundamental difference to the outcome of the genuineness decision, is likely to be unreasonable. If you are aware that documents or evidence have already been submitted and are with another department in the Home Office, you must ask that department for a copy to be forwarded to you[102]."

If the compliance decision states that the parties have not complied, reasons for that decision must be provided[103]. Where there is a legal requirement to give reasons as there is here, there needs to be an adequate explanation of the decision. The essence of the duty to give reasons is whether the information provided by the authority leaves room for 'genuine doubt…as to what has [been] decided and why'[104]. The reasons provided must be intelligible, adequate and proper, and must enable the reader to understand what conclusions were reached on the 'principal important controversial issues'[105]. For example, it will not be enough for the decision to state that a party failed to provide a document, it will need to be explained which document has not been provided and ideally when this was requested. Under the Statutory Guidance a decision that a party has not complied must be made by a Higher Executive Officer (or equivalent) or more senior grade[106].

If it is decided that the parties have complied they will be able to marry or enter a civil partnership after the 70-day period. It is worth noting that an individual served with a s 48 notice can be removed or deported from the UK or leave voluntarily before the compliance question has been

---

102 See page 18

103 s 50(8) Immigration Act 2014

104 *Clarke Homes Ltd v Secretary of State for the Environment* (1993) 66 P & CR 263 [271-272]

105 *South Bucks District Council & Anor v. Porter* [2004] WLR 1953 [36]

106 See page 24

decided. It remains open to the Home Office to decide that such an individual has complied[107].

The parties will not be able to marry or enter a civil partnership if the compliance decision concludes that there has been a failure to comply with the investigation. In order to marry, they would need to give notice to marry again. Practitioners may be aware of cases where couples have been found non-compliant with an investigation and been considered to be in a sham marriage, but have been able to nonetheless marry after giving notice a second time.

It is important to keep in mind that the purpose of the scheme is to detect and determine whether it is more likely than not that a proposed marriage or civil partnership is a sham. Given this, it is peculiar that the scheme allows for a marriage or civil partnership to be prevented where there is non-compliance with an investigation, but not where a sham marriage is found. Of course it is likely that detention or enforcement action will flow from a sham marriage finding and that it is these actions that will prevent the marriage from occurring instead where it is found that there has been compliance.

The marriage referral and investigation scheme does not provide for any appeal or administrative review against a negative compliance decision. Any challenge will need to be by pre-action letter and then a judicial review.

It may well be decided that a couple have complied with the investigation so they are able to marry, but that the relationship is a sham. The Home Office Marriage Investigation Policy Guidance states that the couple must be informed of a sham marriage determination at the same time they are advised of the compliance decision[108]. Proceeding with a

---

[107] The Proposed Marriages and Civil Partnerships (Conduct of Investigations, etc) Regulations 2015, S.I. 2015/397, paras. 17(4)(5)(6)(7)

[108] See page 19.

marriage or civil partnership will not result in any immigration advantage where the evidence proves that it is a sham.

Suitable enforcement action, such as curtailment of leave or removal action, can be taken against individuals that are immigration offenders, if there are reasonable grounds for suspecting a sham marriage or partnership and investigating the relationship and even if there are not. If the Secretary of State determines that the marriage or partnership is a sham, she can of course refuse any immigration application made by a party on the grounds of their relationship. It may of course be the case that the relationship is accepted to be genuine before or after any investigation, but any application is refused on other grounds. The Home Office can seek to prosecute individuals involved in a criminal offence by making contact with a prosecuting authority. An offence might include perjury, facilitating illegal immigration etc. We will consider the consequences of a sham marriage or partnership finding further in Chapter 6.

# CHAPTER FIVE

# MARRIAGE INVESTIGATIONS OUTSIDE THE 2014 SCHEME

The marriage referral and investigation scheme is just one of the ways in which investigations into non-genuine marriages are carried out by the Home Office. Marriage investigations can also occur when individuals make applications to regularise their status, when intelligence in received by the Home Office, when individuals are encountered, or following a criminal investigation. In this chapter we will consider these scenarios.

## 5.1 Applications under Appendix FM of the Immigration Rules

Where an individual makes an application for leave to enter or remain based on a relationship with a British national or settled person the application is made under Appendix FM of the Immigration Rules. Appendix FM requires the parties to show that their relationship is genuine and subsisting[109] and that each party intends to live permanently with the other[110].

As discussed in Chapter 4, there is separate policy guidance for these applications which specifically addresses how the Home Office are to assess and approach sham marriages, i.e., Family Policy: Partners, divorce and dissolution Version 1.0 29 May 2019[111]. This Guidance makes clear that where a relationship has been determined to be a sham as part of the marriage referral and investigation scheme it is expected that an

[109] Appendix FM E-ECP 2.6, E-LTRP 1.7

[110] Appendix FM E-ECP 2.10, E-LTRP 1.10

[111] https://assets.publishing.service.gov.uk/government/uploads/system/uploads/attachment_data/file/835362/Partner_divorce_and_dissolution_guidance_v.1.0ext.pdf see pages 12-20

application made under the immigration rules that relies on the relationship will be refused on genuineness grounds. However, it makes clear that the Secretary of State must consider any new information or evidence that is available as well as any previous determination made. As such, applications should specifically address any sham marriage decisions made against clients and evidence should be gathered which allows for departure from such findings.

It is important to also note that the Guidance suggests that applications will be refused on suitability grounds if a relationship has been determined as bogus in an investigation.

On 1 December 2020, the Immigration Rules were amended. Paragraph 9.6.1. of the Immigration Rules provides that an application for entry clearance, permission to enter and permission to stay may be refused where it is more likely than not that the applicant is, or has been, involved in a sham marriage or sham civil partnership. Paragraph 9.6.2. of the Immigration Rules provides that entry clearance or permission may be cancelled where it is more likely than not that the person is, or has been, involved in a sham marriage or sham civil partnership.[112]

Appendix FM contains a long list of suitability grounds. Immigration Rule S-LTR 2.5 states that an application for leave to remain will normally be refused if the Secretary of State has given notice to the applicant and their partner under section 50(7)(b) of the Immigration Act 2014 that one or both of them have not complied with the investigation of their proposed marriage or civil partnership. Other suitability grounds which may be relevant include (a) an Applicant having failed to comply with a requirement to attend an interview, provide information or provide physical data without reasonable

---

[112] See also Suitability: Sham marriage or civil partnership Version 1.0 2 December 2020

https://assets.publishing.service.gov.uk/government/uploads/system/uploads/attachment_data/file/940779/sham-marriage-v1.0ext.pdf

excuse[113], (b) an Applicant's entry or stay not being conducive to the public good because, for example, the Applicant's conduct (including convictions), character, associations, or other reasons, make it undesirable to grant them leave[114], (c) where false information, false representations or false documents have been submitted in relation to an application (including false information submitted to any person to obtain a document used in support of the application) or there has been a failure to disclose material facts in relation to the application[115].

It is worth noting that an application for entry clearance may be refused if an applicant has previously contrived in a significant way to frustrate the intention of the rules or there are other aggravating circumstances (in addition to an immigration breach)[116]. The Secretary of State's Policy Guidance has long considered taking part, attempting to take part, or facilitating a sham marriage or marriage of convenience to fall under these provisions[117].

In cases where the relationship was not investigated under the referral scheme or where no sham marriage determination was made following a marriage referral investigation despite reasonable suspicions, it remains possible for the Secretary of State to reconsider this issue when deciding an application for leave. The Guidance states that 'if new, significant or compelling information comes to light, in cases where the Home Office strongly suspected that the relationship was a sham or one of convenience at the time of the referral, decision-makers may need to arrange an

---

[113] Appendix FM S-EC 1.6, S-LTR 1.7

[114] Appendix FM S-EC 1.5, S-LTR 1.6

[115] Appendix FM S-EC 2.2, S-LTR 2.2,; See also Part 9 of the Immigration Rules 9.7.3

[116] Part 9 of the Immigration Rules 9.8.2(a)(c)

[117] See for example, General grounds for refusal Section 2 – version 29.0 11 January 2018, p54 (please note this guidance refers to the former Paragraph 320(11) of the Immigration Rules)

interview or make further enquiries with regards to the genuineness of the relationship.'

The Family Policy Guidance usefully sets out factors that the Home Office consider are associated with a genuine and subsisting relationship and those which they consider are not. Factors associated with a couple being in a genuine and subsisting relationship include a couple being able to provide evidence of being in a long-term relationship or a cohabiting relationship, having children and sharing responsibility for them, sharing financial responsibilities (such as joint accounts, utility bills in joint names), parties having visited each other's countries or families[118].

There is a much longer list provided of 'factors which may prompt additional scrutiny'[119]. Additional scrutiny is described as needing to consider whether further information needs to be obtained or the application needs to be investigated further before a decision is made upon the same. The list of factors which may necessitate further enquiries is very extensive. It includes a party having failed to attend an interview without reasonable explanation, an inability to provide information about living arrangements, having no or few family guests or significant family members present at a wedding or reception, inability to communicate in a common language, inability to provide accurate personal details about a partner, an individual having applied for leave in another category unsuccessfully prior to making this application based on their relationship, a party has previously sponsored another individual to be in the UK with them as their partner. It is important practitioners consider this Guidance carefully and advise their clients to address these issues directly in applications for leave to remain if they arise in their cases. The Guidance helpfully reminds caseworkers that they must be sensitive to religious and cultural practices when assessing the genuineness of a relationship. It is noted that in an arranged marriage couples may not have spent much time together prior to the wedding, that for some cultures and faiths marriage is not confirmation of a pre-

[118] Pages 16-17

[119] Pages 17-19

existing relationship but instead the start of a commitment, that pre-marital cohabitation is not accepted in some cultures and religions, that in some cultures correspondence is directed to the male head of the household. Where it appears that the Home Office have failed to apply their own guidance when assessing the genuineness of a relationship, there may be arguments that the decision making is unlawful.[120]

The Home Office can make additional checks with the couple or seek information from other government departments, such as a local authority or the Department of Work and Pensions (DWP). In cases where there are concerns about a party not having capacity[121] to consent to the relationship or marriage owing to learning difficulties for example, the Guidance states that additional scrutiny can involve evidence or an assessment from social services showing the parties had capacity to consent to the marriage.

It is not entirely uncommon for a third party, such as an aggrieved family member, to inform the Home Office that a relationship is not genuine in their opinion. The Family Policy Guidance makes clear that these opinions should not be afforded any weight. However, where there is information from a reliable third party, such as the police or social services or a registration officer or a minister of religion or the forced marriage unit, that a relationship is one of convenience this can be taken into account. The Family Policy Guidance says that it may not be possible for information from a reliable third party to be used in a decision letter. This potentially raises issues of illegality. An Applicant cannot address the issues against them if they are unable to see and/or

---

120 See for example, *Lumba (WL) v Secretary of State for the Home Department* [2011] UKSC 12, [2012] 1 A.C. 245

121 Mental Capacity Act 2005, ss1-3

understand the case against them[122] and it may be important to remind the Home Office of their need to act fairly when making their decisions.

### 5.2 European Applications

On 31 December 2020 the Immigration (European Economic Area) Regulation 2016 ('the EEA Regulations') were revoked and EU free movement ended. As a result, from 1 January 2021, free movement rights under Directive 2004/38/EC cease to have effect in the UK and EEA nationals[123] and their family members will require permission to enter and remain in the UK.

Where an application was submitted under the EEA Regulations on or before 31 December 2020, or where an application for a family permit was submitted validly after 31 December 2020[124] decisions will continue to be made on these pending EEA applications until 30 June 2021. Appeals against refusal of these applications will also continue to be heard[125].

Where an individual makes an application for a right of admission or residence as a family member or extended family member of an EEA

---

[122] See for example *R v Secretary of State for the Home Department, ex p. Doody* [1994] 1 A.C. 531 [560] and *CM (EM country guidance; disclosure) Zimbabwe CG [2013] UKUT 0059* [36-38]

[123] The term EEA nationals means nationals of the countries in the European Economic Area under Directive 2004/38/EC, other than the UK and as well as Switzerland; see EEA Regulations 2016 S.I. 2-16/1052 Regulation 2 'EEA national'. Please note that British citizens/dual nationals can fall within the scope of the EEA Regulations, see for example Regulation 9.

[124] The Immigration and Social Security Co-ordination (EU Withdrawal) Act 2020 (Consequential, Saving, Transitional and Transitory Provisions) (EU Exit) Regulations 2020, S.I. 2020/1309, para 3(2)

[125] The Citizens' Rights (Application Deadline and Temporary Protection) (EU Exit) Regulations 2020, S.I., 2020/1209 and The Immigration and Social Security Co-ordination (EU Withdrawal) Act 2020 (Consequential, Saving, Transitional and Transitory Provisions) (EU Exit) Regulations 2020, S.I., 2020/1309, Schedule 3

national the genuineness of their relationship will be relevant. This is because under Regulation 2 of the EEA Regulations 2016, a spouse, civil partner or durable partner does not include a party to a marriage, civil partnership or durable partnership of convenience.

Again, there is separate Policy Guidance which addresses these applications and the assessment of marriages of convenience within the same, i.e., Free Movement Rights: direct family members of European Economic Area (EEA) nationals guidance Version 9.0 21 February 2020[126].

The Guidance states that if there has been a criminal investigation into the marriage or civil partnership that has resulted in a conviction for any of the parties involved, the EEA application can be refused. If no convictions have been brought against the parties involved but the Home Office still suspect the marriage or civil partnership is one of convenience a four-stage test is set out that must be applied to assess the relationship.

The first step is to consider whether there are factors which indicate that the marriage or partnership is one of convenience. These factors simply mean that further investigation is required they are not sufficient alone to determine the issue of marriage of convenience. The Policy Guidance does not list what these factors are and says that this information is restricted for internal Home Office use. However, the factors set out in the 'Marriage and civil partnership referral and investigation scheme: statutory guidance for Home Office staff March 2015'[127] and Family Policy: Partners, divorce and dissolution Version 1.0 29 May 2019[128] documents are likely to be relevant. It is only if any of the internal risk factors exist that a decision maker would proceed to the second stage.

[126]https://assets.publishing.service.gov.uk/government/uploads/system/uploads/attachment_data/file/867664/free-movement-rights-direct-family-members-of-EEA-nationals-v9.0ext.pdf – see pages 37 to 44

[127] Pages 7-8

[128] Pages 16-19

In EEA cases it is noteworthy that being an immigration overstayer, illegal entrant or an individual in breach of their conditions could be a potential risk factor. It has for some time been established that spouses and civil partners of EEA nationals are able to benefit from EU rights of residence as family members and extended family members despite having poor or adverse immigration histories. In the case of *Blaise Baheten Metock and Others v Minister of Justice, Equality and Law Reform*[129] the European Court of Justice held that national laws which make the rights of admission and residence for a spouse or civil partner of an EEA national dependent upon prior lawful residence in a country were unlawful under Directive 2004/38. These individuals were considered to have rights of entry and residence solely on the basis of their marriage or partnership, irrespective of where and when and how they married, how the individual has entered the UK, or where and how they had lived prior to coming in the UK.

The second stage looks at whether there are factors in the case which would make it difficult to show that the partnership is one of convenience and which would lead to a referral to a senior caseworker. This includes there being a child of the relationship or there being little prospect of a refusal being upheld on appeal when considering all of the evidence. If these factors do not arise or if there are doubts about the authenticity of documents provided, the decision maker is to move on to the third stage.

The third step is to refer a case to a senior caseworker to recommend a marriage interview being carried out. Before a decision is made to refer a case for interview a caseworker can gather more information by, for example, sending a marriage questionnaire to an applicant. A senior caseworker will decide if an interview is appropriate. If they believe it is necessary to interview, the senior caseworker will refer the case to the Permanent Migration Interviewing Team (PMINT).

It is important to note that the Guidance states that the purpose of the interview is to gather facts relating to the relationship and to compare the

[129] Case C-127/08, [2009] All E.R. (EC) 40

parties' knowledge of each other, they should interview the parties separately and ask them the same questions so comparisons can be drawn, the questions should be open where possible, the interviewing officer should review the evidence before any interview and base their questions around this, they must not use set lists of questions. Representatives should consider interview notes and assess whether this Guidance has been followed. Further on in this chapter, there is a separate section on marriage interviews and consideration of some authorities on interviews. This may be of use to representatives in challenges which centre around an interview process.

Interestingly, the Guidance states that home visits for a marriage interview (which can be more intrusive) are only to be requested where an application cannot be resolved in any other way. In EEA cases where a home interview has been requested, practitioners should consider whether this has been as a last resort or not.

Once the PMINT have conducted the interview the case will be passed back for a decision. The fourth and final stage is for the caseworker to make a decision following an interview. The Guidance makes clear that decision makers must consider the factors which led to suspicions, documentary evidence provided by the couple and the interview records. Inconsistencies must be weighed against consistencies and the circumstances of the relationship (i.e., arranged, religious traditions) must be considered. The Guidance states that in-depth knowledge and overall consistency should lead to a positive conclusion in respect of the relationship.

Advisors and clients should be mindful of Regulation 22 of the EEA Regulations 2016. These state that where an applicant or their partner fails to provide additional information requested or fails to attend an interview they are invited to on at least two occasions without good reason, the Secretary of State can draw factual inferences about the applicant's ability to reside under the Regulations as appears appropriate. This can include the inference that the applicant does not have a right to reside under the Regulations. However, a failure to comply with

Regulation 22 should not be the sole basis for such a conclusion. More will be required.

### 5.3 EU Settlement Scheme (EUSS) Applications

As explained above, from 1 January 2021, free movement rights under Directive 2004/38/EC cease to have effect. EEA citizens and their family members require permission to enter and remain in the UK. EEA nationals and spouses, civil partners or unmarried partners of EEA nationals (and Surinder Singh family members of British citizens[130]) are able to apply for entry clearance or status under the EUSS to enable them to enter the UK or to continue to live here post the UK's exit from the European Union, i.e., Appendix EU and Appendix EU (Family Permit) of the Immigration Rules.

Under the EUSS, family member is defined as a spouse or civil partner who is not in a marriage of convenience or a civil partnership of convenience. A durable partner is described as a couple living together in a relationship akin to marriage or civil partnership for at least two years (unless there is other significant evidence of a durable relationship) and it is not a durable partnership of convenience. A durable or civil partnership of convenience and a marriage of convenience are defined under the EUSS as those which are entered into as a means to circumvent criteria a party would have to meet to enjoy a right to enter or reside in the UK or Islands under the EEA Regulations, or any other provision of UK immigration law, or any requirement of the Immigration Rules or under EU or Islands law[131].

Up to and including 30 June 2021, EEA nationals who wish to marry are exempt from the marriage referral and investigation scheme. Further, until this point family members of EEA nationals who hold settled status

---

[130] See *Surinder Singh* Case C-370/90; *O and B v The Netherlands* Case C-456/12; EEA Regulations 2016, Reg 9; Appendix EU and EU Family Permit, Annex 1

[131] Appendix EU and Appendix EU Family Permit, Annex 1 – Definitions

(indefinite leave to enter or remain) under the EUSS are treated as having appropriate immigration status exempting them from the marriage referral and investigation scheme.

The Immigration and Social Security Co-ordination (EU Withdrawal) Act 2020 (Consequential, Saving, Transitional and Transitory Provisions) (EU Exit) Regulations 2020 S.I. 2020/1309 brings EEA citizens, who do not have status under the EUSS or a decision pending on an EUSS application made before 1 July 2021, within scope of the UK's sham marriage referral and investigations scheme. As explained in Chapter 4, from 1 July 2021 British nationals, Irish nationals, EEA nationals and non-EEA nationals with status under the EUSS or a decision pending on an EUSS application submitted before 1 July 2021 are exempt from the sham marriage scheme. EEA citizens, except Irish citizens and those with status under the EUSS or a decision pending on an EUSS application submitted before 1 July 2021, will require a mandatory marriage visitor visa if they are travelling to the UK to marry or form a civil partnership whilst visiting[132].

Being exempt from the marriage referral and investigation scheme, does not however mean that these individuals might not be suspected or found to be in a marriage of convenience. If a family member has a pending application under the EUSS and it is believed that they are in a marriage of convenience, it is likely that investigations will be made and that if a marriage of convenience finding is made their application will be refused and that enforcement action will be considered.

## 5.4 Investigations following Encounters, Enforcement or Tasked Marriage Investigations

The Marriage Investigation Guidance states that the Home Office may investigate a marriage outside of the above circumstances where they receive intelligence or evidence that raises suspicions that a sham marriage

[132] See Appendix V of the Immigration Rules for marriage visitor visa rule

is being planned or has already been carried out. This could occur when an individual is encountered in an enforcement operation or as part of a tasked investigation.

The Marriage Investigation Guidance says that outside of the marriage referral and investigation scheme it is possible to carry out unannounced visits to a residential address to assess whether an offence of breach has been committed. A visit to domestic premises might for example occur when a compliance visit is being carried out to check whether individuals subject to immigration bail are residing at an address in compliance with any bail conditions. A visit to work premises might occur when the home office are checking whether any illegal work is occurring. Individuals can be encountered in street operations which are immigration enforcement led public operations that target locations where intelligence and information indicates that people who are in breach of immigration rules gather at specific locations at certain times. Visits to register offices do still occur, though less than previously owing to the referral scheme under the Immigration Act 2014.

An individual may claim during an encounter that they are in a relationship and that they hold or are eligible for status on this basis. If there are reasonable suspicions about the relationship genuineness, further investigations will be carried out. These can include requesting further evidence. If an immigration offence or breach is reasonably suspected an individual can be arrested administratively and interviewed further. If there are reasonable grounds for suspecting that an immigration criminal offence may have been committed, an immigration officer must seek advice of a Criminal Investigation team (CFI).

There is a separate specific Policy Guidance document which should be referred to if a marriage investigation has occurred through an enforcement visit, see Enforcement Visits Version 3.0 22 December 2020[133]. The document provides guidance on the general conduct and

[133]https://assets.publishing.service.gov.uk/government/uploads/system/uploads/attachment_data/file/947346/enforcement-visits-v3.0ext.pdf

procedures to be followed in enforcement visits and special considerations that must be taken into account. For example, it states that an officer must never remain alone in a room with a suspected immigration offender, they must be clear about the powers they are relying on to seek entry to a premises and whether they are using the same correctly, they must seek to properly identify themselves, where possible visits to households must be conducted with a mixed sex team. The Guidance explains that there constraints on entry by informed consent. For example, in multi-occupancy premises consent must be obtained from the occupier of each room on the premises that is entered and a landlord cannot grant consent for third parties to enter leased premises as consent must be obtained from the tenant or occupier. Further, information about the suspect's status or circumstances must not be volunteered to third parties in premises. Clearly it is important that representatives check that this Policy has been adhered to where relevant, as there may be challenges if it has not.

## 5.5 Criminal Investigations

There is separate policy guidance for criminal investigations of marriages, namely Criminal investigations: sham marriage Version 3.0 15 January 2021.[134] Amongst other things, the Guidance sets out CPS suggested good practice for immigration enforcement and trained and accredited criminal investigators within the Home Office.

See also the Interviewing suspects Version 7.0 February 2020 Guidance[135]. This sets out definition of an interview, the requirements and relevance of the Police and Criminal Evidence (PACE) Codes of Practice, the law surrounding this area, the procedures and safeguards to be followed before, during and after an interview, the use and storage of

[134] https://assets.publishing.service.gov.uk/government/uploads/system/uploads/attachment_data/file/953001/criminal-investigations-sham-marriage-v3.0-gov-uk.pdf

[135] https://assets.publishing.service.gov.uk/government/uploads/system/uploads/attachment_data/file/864940/interviewing-suspects-v7.0.pdf

any tape or digital recordings, note taking in interviews, the use of interpreters and how to address interviewing prisoners.

### 5.6 Marriage Interviews outside of the Referral and Investigation Scheme

We have considered marriage interviews under the referral and investigation scheme at length in Chapter 4. The Statutory Guidance and Regulations set out a number of procedural safeguards that must be followed. For example, under the referral scheme specific notice periods must be given for an interview.

There is guidance on interviews outside of the referral scheme; see the Marriage Investigations Policy Guidance[136]. There are differences. Much of what is set out in respect of EEA applications marriage interviews is relevant but there are some differences and additional issues in the Marriage Investigations Policy Guidance that representatives should consider.

Irrespective of whether an interview is taking place under the referral scheme or not, the purpose of the interview is to assess whether the parties are in a sham marriage. The Guidance explains that interviews must test the understanding and complicity of each party recognising that each may have different reasons for entering the same, parties must be given the opportunity to provide explanations on any credibility points, questions should have regards to religious or cultural issues, officers must avoid asking questions which are intrusive (such as about sex life; however if this information is volunteered it can be recorded).

In the case of *Ait-Rabah, R (on the application of) v The Secretary of State for the Home Department* [2016] EWHC 1099 (Admin) [53-54], the Court considered the part of the Home Office policy which strongly advises against officers asking questions about sex life. Despite the

[136] Pages 26-32

mandatory terms of the Guidance the Court held that there was 'no doubt, certainly in the majority of cases, that to ask a couple at a marriage interview about the details of their sex life would be unjustified and unnecessary. But to enquire simply whether their relationship was or was not a sexual one may well be both pertinent and necessary to an interview about the genuineness of a relationship. The answer to such a question is unlikely to be decisive either way, but it may well be relevant. In my judgment, the Home Office policy does not prevent such a question; what it is aimed at is the asking of unnecessary questions about the details of their sexual relationship. I reject the complaint on this ground.'

The Guidance suggests that there are 'local lists of pre-prepared marriage interview questions' available for officers, but that questioning must be tailored to the answers given and any inconsistencies given should be pursued. Where it appears that an interviewing officer is observing a strict list of questions, has failed to be flexible or follow up a potential inconsistency to give the parties a chance to explain it, this is likely to be contrary to the Guidance. Practitioners may be assisted by the Upper Tribunal decision in *Anjum, R (on the application of) v Entry Clearance Officer, Islamabad (entrepreneur – business expansion – fairness generally)* [2017] UKUT 406 (IAC) which held that 'an immigration interview may be unfair, thereby rendering the resulting decision unlawful, where inflexible structural adherence to prepared questions excludes the spontaneity necessary to repeat or clarify obscure questions and/or to probe or elucidate answers given.'[137]

There is other case law on Home Office interviews which may also be useful to refer to where interviews are proposed and carried out. In *R (Mapah) v Secretary of State for the Home Department* [2003] EWHC 306 (Admin) [62], [2003] Imm. A.R. 49, it noted interpreter problems occur, applicants may not have their own interpreters or representation placing them at disadvantage in identifying translation errors, written records cannot always be literally verbatim, the lack of interview record read back removes a measure of protection against mistakes made in recording by

[137] Headnote ii

the interviewer, tape recording of interview would assist. In *Dirshe, R (on the application of) v Secretary of State for the Home Department* [2005] EWCA Civ 421, [2005] 1 W.L.R. 2685 [14-16] it was said that 'fairness requires that the [interview] procedure should give to the applicant an adequate opportunity to challenge its reliability or adequacy.' These decisions relate to asylum interviews. However, in *Anjum* [2017] UKUT 406 (IAC) [21] the Upper Tribunal said that the general tenor and procedural concerns identified in *Dirshe* applied with a degree of modification and resonated in a Tier 1 Entrepreneur genuineness interview under the immigration rules. Practitioners should consider requesting tape recording of interviews at an early stage and in writing, by reference to these decisions. Helpfully, the Marriage Investigation Guidance suggests that digital recording of interviews can take place alongside written records.

Similarly to interviews under the referral scheme written records of interviews must be completed during the interview, they must be signed and dated by the official that made the record and they must either be verbatim or an account which adequately summarises (please consider the comments in Chapter 4 on the 'adequate summaries' of interviews.) Here, interviewees must be asked to sign records. It is important clients are advised about this and the importance of checking the record or asking it is read back in its entirety in a language they understand. Parties can decline to sign records and if they do this they should explain why, as any refusal will be recorded.

It may well be that there exists both interview records and interview summary sheets in cases. The latter tends to be completed by a Home Office official who carried out a marriage interview and who makes comments, gives opinions or recommendations to a higher official who then makes a decision in the case. In the case *Miah (interviewer's comments: disclosure: fairness)* [2014] UKUT 00515 (IAC) it was held that 'the document enshrining the interviewer's comments – Form ICV.4605 – must be disclosed as a matter of course. An appellant's right to a fair hearing dictates this course.' Much more recently, in the case of *Nimo (appeals: duty of disclosure)* [2020] UKUT 00088 (IAC) it was held that if the interviewer's comments/summary is not relied upon by the Respondent there was no duty to disclose the same. The Upper Tribunal was wrong to hold in *Miah* [2014] UKUT 515 that, in every appeal involving an alleged marriage of convenience, the interviewer's comments in the Secretary of State's form ICD.4605 must be disclosed to the appellant and the Tribunal. No such general requirement is imposed by the respondent's duty of disclosure or by rule 24 of the Tribunal Procedure (First-tier Tribunal) (Immigration and Asylum Chamber) Rules 2014. However, it was found that the duty not to mislead will require the respondent to disclose form ICD.4605, where there is something in it that could materially assist an applicant, but which is not mentioned in the Home Office decision or in the records of interview[138].

As explained above, if an officer has reasonable grounds for suspecting that an immigration criminal offence (e.g., obtaining leave by deception) may have been committed, the Guidance states that they must suspend an interview and seek advice from a Criminal Investigation team. If Criminal Investigation confirm an interest any interview has to be carried out appropriately trained immigration enforcement officer. An individual should be given a criminal caution, arrested and/or detained the person in accordance with the Police and Criminal Evidence Act 1984 (PACE), or equivalent processes in Scotland and Northern Ireland, pending further investigation. This can include a visit to their home address.

In *Ait-Rabah* [2016] EWHC 1099 (Admin) [56] there was an argument advanced by a Claimant, with reliance on Home Office Guidance, that a marriage interview had to be conducted under caution. The Court said that there was no suggestion that PACE applied to that case, but further that the policy on this topic was far from clear as to whether a caution was required. Even if it was, it was considered that it did not invalidate the decisions reached. The representative accepted that a failure to provide a proper caution did not mean that the Court should disregard

[138] Paras 33-36

the answers given in interview, it simply meant there was a need to review with particular care the answers that were provided. In any event, there was in fact no dispute by the Claimant about the accuracy of the answers given.

It is evident that there is scope for challenges to decisions which stem from investigations outside the referral and investigation scheme. In the next chapter, we will consider the decisions that flow from investigations and the opportunities to challenge adverse decisions further.

# CHAPTER SIX

# SHAM MARRIAGE FINDINGS AND CONSEQUENCES

In this final chapter we will look at actions that can be taken after a sham marriage investigation.

## 6.1 Sham Marriage / Marriage of Convenience Findings

As we have repeatedly seen, an investigation will determine whether or not it is considered that an individual

(a) has entered into a sham marriage or a marriage, civil partnership or a durable partnership of convenience,

(b) has attempted to enter into such a marriage or partnership,

(c) has assisted another person to enter into such a marriage or partnership, or

(d) has attempted to assist another individual with such a marriage or partnership.

We will start by looking at the tests to be applied in these cases and how sham marriage findings are arrived at.

### 6.1.1. Burden of Proof

The Supreme Court confirmed, in the decision of *Sadovska,* the well-established principle that the burden of proof for establishing that parties are in a marriage of convenience rests with the Secretary of State[139].

It is useful to consider the Court of Appeal's decision in *Agho* [2015] EWCA Civ 1198 at paragraph 13, which summarised the position on burdens of proof well. Here it was said that 'as a matter of principle a spouse establishes a prima facie case that he or she is a family member of an EEA national by providing the marriage certificate and the spouse's passport; that the legal burden is on the Secretary of State to show that any marriage thus proved is a marriage of convenience; and that that burden is not discharged merely by showing "reasonable suspicion". Of course in the usual way the evidential burden may shift to the applicant by proof of facts which justify the inference that the marriage is not genuine, and the facts giving rise to the inference may include a failure to answer a request for documentary proof of the genuineness of the marriage where grounds for suspicion have been raised.'[140]

In a claim under Appendix FM, the burden of proof in meeting the immigration rules is on the Applicant. This includes in showing that the relationship is genuine and subsisting. If an allegation of deception or dishonesty is made or the general grounds of refusal (which as we have seen in Chapter 5 now specifically include sham marriage or civil

[139] at para. 28.

[140] See also *Papajorgji (EEA spouse – marriage of convenience) Greece* [2012] UKUT 00038 (IAC) at paragraphs 14 and 19 where it was said that 'there is an evidential burden on the respondent. If there is no evidence that could support a conclusion that the marriage is one of convenience, the appellant does not have to deal with the issue. But once the issue is raised, by evidence capable of pointing to a conclusion that the marriage is one of convenience, it is for the appellant to show that his marriage is not one of convenience.'

partnership grounds) are raised, the burden of proof is on the Secretary of State[141].

### 6.1.2 Standard of Proof

The standard of proof is the balance of probabilities[142]. *Papajorgji (EEA spouse – marriage of convenience) Greece* [2012] UKUT 00038 (IAC) at paragraph 39 sets out the position well stating, 'in the light of the totality of the information before me, including the assessment of the claimant's answers and any information provided, am I satisfied that it is more probable than not this is a marriage of convenience?'

### 6.1.3 The Assessment of the Intentions of the Parties

In Chapter 2, we consider the difference between the terms sham marriage and marriage of convenience. We also there look at length at the importance of considering the 'predominant purpose' for the marriage or civil partnership.

In *Rosa v Secretary of State for the Home Department* [2016] EWCA Civ 14 [41] it was held that the parties intentions should be considered by the Secretary of State at the point that they are entering the marriage. It was considered 'useful to contrast a marriage of convenience with a "genuine" marriage.' The Court of Appeal here reminded all that 'the question whether a marriage is "subsisting" looks to whether the marital relationship is a continuing one.'

Much of the policy guidance refers to the need to consider the genuineness of the relationship. Many investigations into marriages are conducted after a marriage or civil partnership has taken place where the

---

141 See for example *Shen (Paper appeals; proving dishonesty)* [2014] UKUT 236 (IAC), [2014] Imm. A.R. 971; *AA (Nigeria) v Secretary of State for the Home Department* [2010] EWCA Civ 773, [2011] 1 W.L.R. 564; *JC (Part 9 HC395, burden of proof) China* [2007] UKAIT 00027; Suitability: Sham marriage or civil partnership Version 1.0 2 December 2020 at page 5

142 *Re B (Children)* [2008] UKHL 35, [2009] 1 AC 11

Home Office are in reality considering the ongoing nature of the relationship, often years after the marriage. Where this arises representatives should remind the Secretary of State of *Rosa*.

The subsistence of the marriage can of course shed much light on the parties intentions when it was entered. Equally relationships change. As Richards LJ recognised in *Rosa,* 'a marriage of convenience might turn into a genuine marriage in the course of time'[143]. There can of course be very difficult periods which can include separations. This may well be no reflection of the parties intentions when they entered their marriage or partnership.

Representatives are reminded that it is long established that the separated spouse or civil partner of an EEA national exercising their free movement rights is entitled to reside in the UK even after separation, provided they both remain in the UK[144]. This remains relevant to EEA cases and Appendix EU cases.

Under the Immigration Rules the situation is different; an applicant must continue to show they are in a genuine and subsisting relationship to have their leave extended.

### 6.1.4 The Circumstances of the Investigation and Evidence

In chapters 4 and 5 we have considered the procedures to be followed in investigations and the evidence that is likely to be considered by the Secretary of State. It is worth considering how the authorities have approached investigations.

In *Sadovska*, Mr Malik a Pakistani national who overstayed his leave, gave notice of intention to marry Ms Sadovska, a Lithuanian national who held permanent residency. On the day of their wedding immigration officers came to the Registrar's Office and interviewed them under

---

[143] Para. 41

[144] *Diatta v Land Berlin* [1985] E.C.R. 567

caution in English. They were both detained and issued with removal papers which carried appeal rights. In their appeals they complained 'that their interviews were unfair, oppressive and repugnant to public law standards. The circumstances of being approached on their wedding day by uniformed immigration officers carrying batons and handcuffs meant that they were frightened. They agreed to be interviewed in English but neither [was] fluent in English. They had no time to contact their solicitor for advice, to obtain an interpreter, to produce evidence and contact witnesses. They complained that both the First-tier and the Upper Tribunal had thought the interviews were of central importance, yet they gave no weight to the circumstances in which they had taken place.'[145] In remitting their appeals back to the First-Tier Tribunal, the Supreme Court said that in looking at the couple's discrepancies in their interviews 'the circumstances in which the interviews took place… must be borne fully in mind. Furthermore, there were many matters on which their accounts were consistent.'[146]

*Agho v The Secretary of State for the Home Department* [2015] EWCA Civ 1198 can be helpful where there is an unannounced visit to a couple at their home. Here, a Nigerian national made an application for a residence card as the family member of an EEA national. It appeared that there was an unannounced visit to a residential address by a police officer on the Home Office's request. The officer attended the premises at 7.30pm, he made a file note of speaking to a female visitor at the premises who denied knowledge of other occupants, he left a note advising he would be reporting the premises to the local authority for multiple occupancy, he noted that the next day the managing agents advised him by phone that they knew no tenants by the names of Collin or Kozo. This note and visit lead the Home Office to believe that the couple did not live together at the address and that their marriage was one of convenience. The note was not produced until the day of the hearing. This was considered to be

[145] Para. 19

[146] Para. 34

unfair[147]. It was found that the failure to put the marriage of convenience allegation to the parties prior to a decision being made was a clear breach of good practice.[148] The Court of Appeal considered that the fact that the parties were not at home when the officer visited established nothing: 'there was nothing unusual about people not being at home at 7:30 in the evening', the lady who he met was simply a visitor, the note was full of obscurities and it was not clear from the note what the officer had actually said in the note he left or what communications had been had following that[149]. It was considered that this 'late-disclosed, second-hand and confused evidence', which was the totality of the evidence relied upon by the Secretary of State, was not sufficient a serious marriage of convenience finding which was in any event contrary to the documentary evidence relating to cohabitation[150].

The above decisions, and chapters 4 and 5 of this book, demonstrate the importance of considering the fairness of the investigation when challenging sham marriage findings.

## 6.2 The Consequences

Where the Secretary of State has concluded that the marriage is a sham there are a number of actions that she might take. This can include (a) refusal of leave to enter or remain, (b) cancellation or curtailment of leave, (c) prosecution of individuals.

---

147 Para 22

148 Para. 5; *Papajorgji (EEA spouse – marriage of convenience) Greece* [2012] UKUT 00038 (IAC) [27] "…[w]here there is such suspicion the matter requires further investigation and the claimant should be invited to respond to the basis of suspicion by producing evidential material to dispel it."

149 Para. 40

150 Paras. 41, 45

### 6.2.1 The Secretary of State's Discretion

It is important to note that it is not compulsory for an application to be refused or leave to be curtailed after a sham marriage determination; this is always a discretionary decision.

It may not always be proportionate or reasonable to take action. Representatives are again reminded of Lady Hale's comments in *Sadovska* that 'a marriage cannot be considered as a marriage of convenience simply because it brings an immigration advantage, or indeed any other advantage (for example the right to a particular surname, location-related allowances, tax advantages or entitlement to social housing for married couples).'[151] Practitioners may be reading these words and considering that if a genuine couple are predominantly marrying to claim social housing benefits or to seek tax relief which they would otherwise not be entitled to, what is the real difference between this and the genuine couple marrying for an immigration advantage. Is refusal or cancellation of leave proportionate in these circumstances?

The parties to the marriage or civil partnership may not face the same action. Each individual may have different intentions and this must be considered with care. Furthermore, each individual's own rights and the extent of their life in the UK may result in different outcomes. This was a point considered again in the Supreme Court's decision in *Sadovska*, where the Lady Hale said that 'a non-EU national may be guilty of abuse when the EU national is not, because she believes that it is a genuine relationship… In the case of a person exercising EU law rights, the tribunal must also be satisfied that the removal would be a proportionate response to the abuse of rights established. So it would be one thing to find that the proposed marriage had been shown to be one of convenience, and therefore that it was right to prevent it, but quite another thing to find that expelling Ms Sadovska from the country where

[151] Para. 29

she had lived and worked for so long and had other family members living was a proportionate response to that.'[152]

In cases under Appendix FM and outside of the immigration rules, the Secretary of State will have to have regard to family and private life rights under Article 8 ECHR. She must have regard to her duties to consider the best interests of any minor children under Section 55 of the Borders Citizenship and Immigration Act 2009 and Article 3 of the UN Convention on the Rights of the Child, and whether there are any exceptional, compelling or compassionate circumstances. Practitioners will need to consider whether the Secretary of State has actually exercised discretion, whether she has had regard to all available evidence and facts and whether the decision is proportionate. It may be useful to refer to the Home Office Suitability: Sham marriage or civil partnership Guidance if it is felt that discretion has not been exercised[153]. As was said in *R (Agyarko) v SSHD* [2017] UKSC 11, [2017] 1 W.L.R. 823 'the ultimate question is how a fair balance should be struck between the competing public and individual interests involved, applying a proportionality test.'[154]

### 6.2.2 Refusals of Applications under the Immigration Rules / EEA Applications

If an applicant has an application outstanding or later makes an application based on the assessed relationship under the immigration rules, it is likely that it will be refused on the grounds of genuineness and suitability.

Most decisions refusing leave to remain will carry an in-country right of appeal to the First-Tier Tribunal Immigration and Asylum Chamber[155].

---

[152] Paras. 29-30

[153] Version 1.0 2 December 2020 at pages 7-8

[154] Para. 60

[155] Nationality, Immigration and Asylum Act 2002, s 82

If a claim is certified as clearly unfounded[156], that can be challenged by way of judicial review.

Where you have a certified decision it may be useful to refer to the Respondent's Certification of Protection and human rights claim under section 94 of the Nationality, Immigration and Asylum Act 2002 (clearly unfounded claims) Version 4.0 12 February 2019 which says that deception is a credibility point and credibility should not be taken into account when considering whether to certify a claim unless the caseworker is satisfied that nobody could believe the claimant's account that they did not use deception[157]. This part of the guidance came after the decision in *Ahsan v SSHD* [2017] EWCA Civ 2009, [2018] Imm. A.R. 531, where the Court said they 'would be reluctant to accept that it was possible fairly to determine an allegation of this character – that is, an allegation of deliberate dishonesty, with serious implications for the Appellants' rights and reputation – without them being given the opportunity to give oral evidence in rebuttal... For those reasons [they were] not persuaded that [the Secretary of State had] any answer to the Appellants' case that an out-of-country appeal would not satisfy the procedural requirements of article 8. Such a breach of the Appellants' rights can be avoided by allowing them to challenge the removal decisions in their cases by way of judicial review.'[158]

EEA or EUSS applicants who have applications which depend upon a marriage or partnership are also likely to see these will be refused. Again, these refusals will carry a right of appeal[159].

---

[156] Ibid. ss 92, 94; *FR & Anor (Albania), R v SSHD* [2016] EWCA Civ 605, [2016] Imm. A.R. 1341

[157] https://assets.publishing.service.gov.uk/government/uploads/system/uploads/attachment_data/file/919737/certification-s94-guidance-0219.pdf, Pages 13-14

[158] Paras. 91 and 92

[159] The Immigration (European Economic Area) Regulations 2016, S.I. 2016; The Immigration (Citizens' Rights Appeals) (EU Exit) Regulations 2020, S.I. 2020 No. 61; The Citizens' Rights (Application Deadline and Temporary Protection) (EU Exit) Regulations 2020, S.I. 2020/1209; Immigration and Social Security Co-ordination

Practitioners should note *R (Bilal Ahmed) v SSHD(EEA/s 10 appeal rights: effect) IJR* [2015] UKUT 00436 (IAC), [2015] Imm. A.R. 1320 where it was held that 'where a non-EEA national spouse or civil partner is suspected of being party to a marriage of convenience, and they have not previously had issued to them a document under the EEA Regulations, they are not considered to be a family member of an EEA national for the purposes of the EEA Regulations. The refusal of a document will take place under the EEA Regulations, but they will be removed under section 10 of the Immigration and Asylum Act 1999.' We look at this a little more below. However, whilst these individuals can 'bring their appeal in the UK against the refusal to issue them with a document under the EEA Regulations, this is non-suspensive of removal.' The correctness of this approach was confirmed by the decision of the Court of Appeal in *Ahmed, R (On the Application Of) v SSHD* [2016] EWCA Civ 303, [2016] Imm. A.R. 869.

In considering *Ahmed,* representatives may wish to consider the fairness of an individual challenging allegations of a marriage of convenience in an appeal whilst they are outside of the UK. In Ahsan the Court of Appeal said that they 'would be reluctant to accept that it was possible fairly to determine an allegation of this character – that is, an allegation of deliberate dishonesty, with serious implications for the Appellants' rights and reputation – without them being given the opportunity to give oral evidence in rebuttal.' In *Kiarie and Byndloss, R (on the applications of) v Secretary of State for the Home Department* [2017] UKSC 42, [2017] 1 W.L.R. 2380 the Supreme Court discussed the 'practical limitations' of appeals where Appellants were out of the country. This included the use of video link particularly in the First-tier Tribunal, the lack of facilities in some centres, competing demands from other priorities (such as bail hearings), the need for compatibility with overseas equipment, the need for the appellant to bear the costs, the need to co-ordinate timings with appeal hearings, the formidable difficulties that Appellants would face in instructing their lawyers and the insurmountable difficulties that would

(EU Withdrawal) Act 2020 (Consequential, Saving, Transitional and Transitory Provisions) (EU Exit) Regulations 2020, S.I., 2020/1309

be faced in obtaining any necessary supporting professional expert evidence.

Individuals are 'entitled to an appeal where the facts and circumstances must be fully investigated. That must mean, as held in *Papajorgji*, that the tribunal has to form its own view of the facts from the evidence presented.'[160]

It is useful for clients to have regard to the genuine relationship factors set out in the Appendix FM Family policy (discussed in chapter 5) when preparing documentary evidence.

In *Papagorji*, the parties were found not to be in a marriage of convenience where the marriage had (a) not been contracted shortly before an application for entry clearance, (b) lasted some 12 years at the date of decision, and (c) the application revealed that both husband and wife lived at the same address, shared a common telephone number and that there were children of the marriage. The Tribunal said that 'a durable marriage with children and co-habitation is quite inconsistent with [the] definition [of a marriage of convenience.' [161]

In *Rosa* inconsistent evidence before the Tribunal as to when the parties met, whether family attended their wedding, whether they had lived together, whether the wife had visited her husband in prison were found to support the conclusion that the marriage was one of convenience. The absence of witnesses at a hearing who had written witness statements was an adverse factor. Further, the lack of a tenancy agreement to support cohabitation was considered significant. Indeed, it was noted that it was in any event easy to change a postal address.[162]

Where there is Home Office reliance on the ease at which a postal address can be changed, *Agho* may be of use. Here the Court noted that it was of

---

160 *Sadovska v SSHD* [2017] UKSC 54 [2017] 1 W.L.R. 2926, para.28

161 Para. 29

162 Paras. 34-36

course possible for a postal address to be set up as part of an elaborate system under which an individual enters into a sham tenancy agreement and a series of official documents can be sent to parties at a leased address while they live elsewhere. But where the documents are sufficiently numerous, and various in their character, it was felt that compelling evidence of such a deception would be required. Underhill LJ said that the supposed deception would be all the more odd if a party was making substantial payments to the landlord.[163]

### 6.2.3 Enforcement Decisions – Curtailment of Leave / Cancellation of Leave under the Immigration Acts / Administrative Removal / Deportation

The enforcement action that can be taken once a finding is made that a marriage is bogus depends upon the immigration status of the parties and the point at which their conduct with the marriage is assessed.

If a party to a sham marriage requires leave to enter or remain in the UK but does not have it, the Secretary of State can carry out removal action in accordance with Section 10 of the Immigration and Asylum Act 1999 as amended by Part 1, Section 1, of the Immigration Act 2014.

Where extant leave to enter or remain, such as work or student leave or leave under Appendix FM as a family member, is curtailed, cancelled, revoked[164], a simultaneous decision can be made to remove under Section 10 of the Immigration and Asylum Act 1999.

The stage at which the relevant conduct occurred is relevant for EEA and EUSS cases as a result of the Agreement on the withdrawal of the United Kingdom of Great Britain and Northern Ireland from the European Union and the European Atomic Energy Community (19 October 2019). Article 20 states that 'The conduct of Union citizens or United

---

[163] Para. 38

[164] Immigration Act 1971, s3(3), s4; Immigration (Leave to Enter or Remain) Order 2000, art.13; Nationality, Immigration and Asylum Act 2002, s 76(2); Part 9 of the Immigration Rules, paragraph 9.6.2

Kingdom nationals, their family members, and other persons, who exercise rights under this Title, where that conduct occurred before the end of the transition period, shall be considered in accordance with Chapter VI of Directive 2004/38/EC. The conduct of Union citizens or United Kingdom nationals, their family members, and other persons, who exercise rights under this Title, where that conduct occurred after the end of the transition period, may constitute grounds for restricting the right of residence by the host State or the right of entry in the State of work in accordance with national legislation. The host State or the State of work may adopt the necessary measures to refuse, terminate or withdraw any right conferred by this Title in the case of the abuse of those rights or fraud, as set out in Article 35 of Directive 2004/38/EC.'

Accordingly, if the marriage of convenience conduct occurred before 11pm on 31 December 2020 individuals will benefit from enhanced protection under the Directive. However, for conduct from 1 January 2021, individuals will be treated less favourably.

Article 35 of Directive 2004/38/EC states that 'Member States may adopt the necessary measures to refuse, terminate or withdraw any right conferred by this Directive in the case of abuse of rights or fraud, such as marriages of convenience. Any such measure shall be proportionate and subject to the procedural safeguards provided for in Articles 30 and 31. Regulation 23 of the EEA Regulations 2016 prevents the admission of an individual to the UK if there are reasonable grounds to suspect that their admission would lead to the misuse of a right of residence. A EEA national and/or their family member can be removed if they have misused their rights or their removal is justified on the grounds of public policy. Under Regulation 26 the misuse of a right to reside occurs when a person observes the requirements of the Regulations in circumstances which do not achieve the purpose of the Regulations and intends to obtain an advantage from the Regulations by engaging in conduct which artificially creates the conditions required to satisfy the criteria set out in the Regulations. An EEA decision on the grounds of misuse of rights can be taken where there are reasonable grounds to suspect the misuse of a right to reside and it is proportionate to do so.[165]

For conduct that occurred before the end of the transition period, Regulation 27 and Schedule 1 of the EEA Regulations 2016 set out the principles to be considered when making a decision to refuse admission, exclude, refuse or revoke residence or remove an EEA national or their family member from the UK on grounds of public policy or public security. Decisions must be in accordance with the principle of proportionality, based exclusively on the personal conduct of the person, the personal conduct must represent a genuine, present and sufficiently serious threat to one of the fundamental interests of society, matters isolated from particulars of the case or of general prevention do not justify a decision, a decision can be taken on preventative grounds but the grounds must be specific to the person. Considerations include age, state of health, family and economic situation, length of residence, social & cultural integration. There are higher thresholds for the removal of certain EEA nationals and their family members based on their length of residence in the UK. For individuals with a right of permanent residence, decisions must be based on serious grounds of public policy or public security. For EEA nationals and family member with 10 years residence, decisions are only permitted on imperative grounds of public security.

For conduct that has occurred post the transition period, individuals will be subject to far lower thresholds for exclusion and deportation. The test will simply be whether their removal is conducive to the public good[166].

---

[165] Also see Appendix EU, Immigration Rule EU16

[166] The Immigration (European Economic Area) Regulations 2016, S.I. 2016, Regulation 27A; The Citizens' Rights (Application Deadline and Temporary Protection) (EU Exit) Regulations 2020, S.I. 2020/1209, Regulation 7; Appendix EU, Immigration Rule EU16; EU Settlement Scheme: suitability requirements Version 4.0 31 December 2020 – https://assets.publishing.service.gov.uk/government/uploads/system/uploads/attachment_data/file/948009/euss-suitability-v4.0ext.pdf ; Exclusion from the UK Version 4.0 31 December 2020 –

An individual who is an EEA national or holds status as the family member of an EEA national, or who does not hold EUSS leave but has an application pending or is eligible to apply under the EUSS scheme until 30 June 2021 may face enforcement action on the grounds of public policy if their conduct was pre-31 December 2020[167]. If however their conduct was post-31 December 2020, they may face enforcement action under the lower threshold of conducive grounds[168].

Where an individual has leave under EUSS (pre-settled or settled), if their conduct was pre-31 December 2020 they may again face enforcement action on the grounds of public policy[169]. However, if the conduct was post-31 December 2020 they may face curtailment or revocation[170] of their EUSS leave on the grounds of deception or marriage of convenience and thereafter administrative removal under Section 10 of the Immigration and Asylum Act 1999.

Where an individual holds leave as a service provider from Switzerland or an S2 Healthcare visitor any involvement in a bogus marriage is likely to be as a facilitator. If their conduct was pre-31 December 2020 they may again face enforcement action on the grounds of public policy[171]. However, if the conduct was post-31 December 2020 they may face cancellation[172] of their leave on conducive grounds and thereafter

---

https://assets.publishing.service.gov.uk/government/uploads/system/uploads/attachment_data/file/948096/exclusion-v4.0ext.pdf

[167] EEA Regulations 2016, Regulations 23(6)(b) and 27

[168] Ibid. Regulations 23(6)(b) and 27A

[169] Ibid. Regulations 23(6)(b) and 27

[170] Annex 3 Appendix EU, paragraphs A3.3-3.4; Nationality Immigration and Asylum Act 2002, s 76(2);

[171] Regulations 23(6)(b) and 27 of the EEA Regulations 2016

[172] Appendix Service Providers from Switzerland, para. SPS 9.1(b); Appendix H2 Healthcare Visitor, para. HV 11.1(b)

administrative removal under Section 10 of the Immigration and Asylum Act 1999.

Where an individual holds leave as a frontier worker any involvement is again likely to be as a facilitator. If their conduct was pre-31 December 2020 they may again face enforcement action on the grounds of public policy[173]. However, if the conduct was post-31 December 2020 they may be referred to migrant criminality policy before any action is taken.

When enforcement action is taken individual may have appeal rights to exhaust or rights to administrative or judicial review[174]. Whilst the intricacies and complexities of appeals and judicial reviews are beyond the scope of this book, the material within these chapters will assist with appeal preparation and judicial review challenges,

### 6.2.4 Prosecution

As discussed elsewhere in this book, the Home Office can seek the prosecution of those involved in a criminal offence related to the sham marriage, for example perjury or facilitation of illegal immigration, liaising with the relevant prosecuting authority

The main types of offences relating to sham marriages and civil partnerships are facilitation (assisting people to enter, transit or be the

---

[173] The Citizens' Rights (Frontier Workers) (EU Exit) Regulations 2020, Regulations 15(1)(b), 18

[174] See Right of Appeal Version 10.0 18 December 2020 – https://assets.publishing.service.gov.uk/government/uploads/system/uploads/attachment_data/file/946780/rights-of-appeal-v10.pdf ; Judicial Reviews and Injunctions Version 20.0 10 October 2019 – https://assets.publishing.service.gov.uk/government/uploads/system/uploads/attachment_data/file/919646/chapter-60-judicial-reviews_v20.0ext.pdf ; Returns: case consideration Version 1.0 10 February 2017 – https://assets.publishing.service.gov.uk/government/uploads/system/uploads/attachment_data/file/591504/Returns-consideration_v1.0.pdf

UK illegally)[175], conspiracy to facilitate[176], deception[177], bigamy[178], perjury[179], securing or seeking to secure the avoidance, postponement or revocation of enforcement action[180].

Where an individual has a conviction for a sham marriage related offence, the Secretary of State will consider whether refusal and removal is appropriate on the grounds of criminality. The Home Office will consider deportation of foreign criminals. The tests that apply will depend on the individual's immigration status and the date of the relevant conduct as explained above.

In summary, where conduct post-dates 31 December 2020 facing deportation domestic laws apply[181]. An individual who is subject to imprisonment for four years or more deportation will occur unless there are very compelling circumstances; for those who have been sentenced to between 1 year and 4 years imprisonment deportation will occur unless the family life exceptions in the rules are engaged (i.e., it is unduly harsh for a qualifying child or partner) or their private life is engaged (i.e., this includes showing that they have lived here lawfully for more than half their life, they are socially and culturally integrated in the UK and there are very significant obstacles to their integration in their home country, or there are very compelling circumstances. For those subject to less than 1 year imprisonment whose conduct is non-persistent and has caused no serious harm they may still be deported if this is considered conducive to the public good.

---

175 Section 25 Immigration Act 1971

176 Section 1A Criminal Law Act 1977

177 Immigration Act 1971, s24A(1)(a); The Fraud Act 2006

178 Offences against the Person Act 1861, s57

179 Perjury Act 1911, s3

180 Immigration Act 1971, s24A(1)(b)

181 Nationality, Immigration and Asylum Act 2002, Part 5A; Immigration Act 1971, s3(5)

It can be seen from the above that the consequences of a sham marriage or marriage of convenience finding can be far-reaching and catastrophic for individuals. As such, it is imperative that investigations are carried out lawfully, that the correct tests are applied when findings are made, that evidence is prepared meticulously and that challenges are brought against flawed decisions. It is hoped that this book will assist you in dealing with these often tricky and challenging cases.

| |
|---|
| 'Covid-19, Homeworking and the Law – The Essential Guide to Employment and GDPR Issues' by Forbes Solicitors |
| 'Covid-19, Force Majeure and Frustration of Contracts – The Essential Guide' by Keith Markham |
| 'Covid-19 and Criminal Law – The Essential Guide' by Ramya Nagesh |
| 'Covid-19 and Family Law in England and Wales – The Essential Guide' by Safda Mahmood |
| 'A Practical Guide to the Law of Unlawful Eviction and Harassment – 2nd Edition' by Stephanie Lovegrove |
| 'Covid-19, Residential Property, Equity Release and Enfranchisement – The Essential Guide' by Paul Sams and Louise Uphill |
| 'Covid-19, Brexit and the Law of Commercial Leases – The Essential Guide' by Mark Shelton |
| 'A Practical Guide to Costs in Personal Injury Claims – 2nd Edition' by Matthew Hoe |
| 'A Practical Guide to the General Data Protection Regulation (GDPR) – 2nd Edition' by Keith Markham |
| 'Ellis on Credit Hire – Sixth Edition' by Aidan Ellis & Tim Kevan |
| 'A Practical Guide to Working with Litigants in Person and McKenzie Friends in Family Cases' by Stuart Barlow |
| 'Protecting Unregistered Brands: A Practical Guide to the Law of Passing Off' by Lorna Brazell |
| 'A Practical Guide to Secondary Liability and Joint Enterprise Post-Jogee' by Joanne Cecil & James Mehigan |
| 'A Practical Guide to the Pre-Action RTA Claims Protocol for Personal Injury Lawyers' by Antonia Ford |
| 'A Practical Guide to Neighbour Disputes and the Law' by Alexander Walsh |
| 'A Practical Guide to Forfeiture of Leases' by Mark Shelton |
| 'A Practical Guide to Coercive Control for Legal Practitioners and Victims' by Rachel Horman |

| |
|---|
| 'A Practical Guide to Rights Over Airspace and Subsoil' by Daniel Gatty |
| 'Tackling Disclosure in the Criminal Courts – A Practitioner's Guide' by Narita Bahra QC & Don Ramble |
| 'A Practical Guide to the Law of Driverless Cars – Second Edition' by Alex Glassbrook, Emma Northey & Scarlett Milligan |
| 'A Practical Guide to TOLATA Claims' by Greg Williams |
| 'Artificial Intelligence – The Practical Legal Issues' by John Buyers |
| 'A Practical Guide to the Law of Prescription in Scotland' by Andrew Foyle |
| 'A Practical Guide to the Construction and Rectification of Wills and Trust Instruments' by Edward Hewitt |
| 'A Practical Guide to the Law of Bullying and Harassment in the Workplace' by Philip Hyland |
| 'How to Be a Freelance Solicitor: A Practical Guide to the SRA-Regulated Freelance Solicitor Model' by Paul Bennett |
| 'A Practical Guide to Prison Injury Claims' by Malcolm Johnson |
| 'A Practical Guide to the Small Claims Track' by Dominic Bright |
| 'A Practical Guide to Advising Clients at the Police Station' by Colin Stephen McKeown-Beaumont |
| 'A Practical Guide to Antisocial Behaviour Injunctions' by Iain Wightwick |
| 'Practical Mediation: A Guide for Mediators, Advocates, Advisers, Lawyers, and Students in Civil, Commercial, Business, Property, Workplace, and Employment Cases' by Jonathan Dingle with John Sephton |
| 'The Mini-Pupillage Workbook' by David Boyle |
| 'A Practical Guide to Crofting Law' by Brian Inkster |
| 'A Practical Guide to Spousal Maintenance' by Liz Cowell |
| 'A Practical Guide to the Law of Domain Names and Cybersquatting' by Andrew Clemson |
| 'A Practical Guide to the Law of Gender Pay Gap Reporting' by Harini Iyengar |

| |
|---|
| 'A Practical Guide to the Rights of Grandparents in Children Proceedings' by Stuart Barlow |
| 'NHS Whistleblowing and the Law' by Joseph England |
| 'Employment Law and the Gig Economy' by Nigel Mackay & Annie Powell |
| 'A Practical Guide to Noise Induced Hearing Loss (NIHL) Claims' by Andrew Mckie, Ian Skeate, Gareth McAloon |
| 'An Introduction to Beauty Negligence Claims – A Practical Guide for the Personal Injury Practitioner' by Greg Almond |
| 'Intercompany Agreements for Transfer Pricing Compliance' by Paul Sutton |
| 'Zen and the Art of Mediation' by Martin Plowman |
| 'A Practical Guide to the SRA Principles, Individual and Law Firm Codes of Conduct 2019 – What Every Law Firm Needs to Know' by Paul Bennett |
| 'A Practical Guide to Adoption for Family Lawyers' by Graham Pegg |
| 'A Practical Guide to Industrial Disease Claims' by Andrew Mckie & Ian Skeate |
| 'A Practical Guide to Redundancy' by Philip Hyland |
| 'A Practical Guide to Vicarious Liability' by Mariel Irvine |
| 'A Practical Guide to Applications for Landlord's Consent and Variation of Leases' by Mark Shelton |
| 'A Practical Guide to Relief from Sanctions Post-Mitchell and Denton' by Peter Causton |
| 'A Practical Guide to Equity Release for Advisors' by Paul Sams |
| 'A Practical Guide to the Law Relating to Food' by Ian Thomas |
| 'A Practical Guide to Financial Services Claims' by Chris Hegarty |
| 'The Law of Houses in Multiple Occupation: A Practical Guide to HMO Proceedings' by Julian Hunt |
| 'A Practical Guide to Unlawful Eviction and Harassment' by Stephanie Lovegrove |
| 'Occupiers, Highways and Defective Premises Claims: A Practical Guide Post-Jackson – 2nd Edition' by Andrew Mckie |

| |
|---|
| ‘A Practical Guide to Financial Ombudsman Service Claims’ by Adam Temple & Robert Scrivenor |
| 'A Practical Guide to Advising Schools on Employment Law' by Jonathan Holden |
| ‘A Practical Guide to Running Housing Disrepair and Cavity Wall Claims: 2nd Edition’ by Andrew Mckie & Ian Skeate |
| ‘A Practical Guide to Holiday Sickness Claims – 2nd Edition’ by Andrew Mckie & Ian Skeate |
| ‘Arguments and Tactics for Personal Injury and Clinical Negligence Claims’ by Dorian Williams |
| ‘A Practical Guide to Drone Law’ by Rufus Ballaster, Andrew Firman, Eleanor Clot |
| ‘A Practical Guide to Compliance for Personal Injury Firms Working With Claims Management Companies’ by Paul Bennett |
| ‘A Practical Guide to Dog Law for Owners and Others’ by Andrea Pitt |
| ‘RTA Allegations of Fraud in a Post-Jackson Era: The Handbook – 2nd Edition’ by Andrew Mckie |
| ‘RTA Personal Injury Claims: A Practical Guide Post-Jackson’ by Andrew Mckie |
| ‘On Experts: CPR35 for Lawyers and Experts’ by David Boyle |
| ‘An Introduction to Personal Injury Law’ by David Boyle |
| ‘A Practical Guide to Subtle Brain Injury Claims’ by Pankaj Madan |

These books and more are available to order online direct from the publisher at www.lawbriefpublishing.com, where you can also read free sample chapters. For any queries, contact us on 0844 587 2383 or mail@lawbriefpublishing.com.

Our books are also usually in stock at www.amazon.co.uk with free next day delivery for Prime members, and at good legal bookshops such as Wildy & Sons.

We are regularly launching new books in our series of practical day-to-day practitioners' guides. Visit our website and join our free newsletter to be kept informed and to receive special offers, free chapters, etc.

You can also follow us on Twitter at www.twitter.com/lawbriefpub.

www.ingramcontent.com/pod-product-compliance
Lightning Source LLC
LaVergne TN
LVHW022310200926
848481LV00004B/1264
*9781912687930*